Mohammed Sani Garba

My Hedgehogs

AF526017

Mohammed Sani Garba

My Hedgehogs

a holiday memoir

JustFiction Edition

Imprint
Any brand names and product names mentioned in this book are subject to trademark, brand or patent protection and are trademarks or registered trademarks of their respective holders. The use of brand names, product names, common names, trade names, product descriptions etc. even without a particular marking in this work is in no way to be construed to mean that such names may be regarded as unrestricted in respect of trademark and brand protection legislation and could thus be used by anyone.

Cover image: www.ingimage.com

Publisher:
JustFiction! Edition
is a trademark of
Dodo Books Indian Ocean Ltd., member of the OmniScriptum S.R.L Publishing group
str. A.Russo 15, of. 61, Chisinau-2068, Republic of Moldova Europe
Printed at: see last page
ISBN: 978-620-3-57863-8

Copyright © Mohammed Sani Garba
Copyright © 2022 Dodo Books Indian Ocean Ltd., member of the OmniScriptum S.R.L Publishing group

Acknowledgement

I sincerely like to acknowledge most especially those that contributed in making me to successfully write this book. The book is important to me as it reminds me of my past and the paste of some of my relatives, friends and some towns and cities that are part of my life. I am grateful to my guides such as Late Malam Barau the historians and custodians of our community culture Late Shantali Abdullahi Lawal, Shantali Manu Abdullahi, Honourable Urwatu Barau, Galadima Hamza Galadima and many of these historians and custodians of our culture.

Also I like to extend my thanks to my effective editor Ekaterina Efocsa and other editorial team that make my work to yet another standard and making it more acceptable to the audience. Lastly, I thank Dr Mahmud Imam of Chemistry Department, College of Science and Technology of Kaduna Polytechnic, Kaduna Nigeria. He showed me his Chemistry book as his cataloguer, indexer and general editor. This time published by world class international publisher Omniscriptum or specifically Scholar's press. I was really impressed and then as a Writer Scum Librarian I became interested here I am publishing with the scholar's press even though I am a student. I thank you. The last but not the least I thank God who inspired and taught man what he knew not. Those that I forgot to mention and will one day come to read this book please do not be offended to err is man. I appreciate you and appreciate most sincerely your efforts for lifting my career.

Prologue

Our village where my father came from is in the Northern far area of Nigeria. It is sandy unlike the southern Nigeria where it is mostly swampy and full of tick forest. It is when you rich Katsina city, the capital of Katsina state today that you will follow Eastward through Kofar Marusa gate to our village called Matsai. It is here that I enjoyed visiting especially when I was small upto when I was in College and always. Life in the wild and among my grandparents and kinsmen was interesting and superb. I ate what I want and played the way I wanted. Moreover, I entered bush and followed birds, climbed trees, rode on horses and donkeys as well. I became a bush boy and adventurist.

My senior grandfather Galadima Suleiman always was on my side and made sure that I enjoy my stay in the village. So far he was the most senior among my father's descendants in the village. Eventhough, I was small to be told many issues and family lineage history, he never minds to tell me whenever it was evening time when I went to his quarters while his horse tightened eating its foods Galadima will continue narrating sensitive issues to me. Whenever I was on holiday I use to be a favorite of the house and the young ones my age in the village will be attracted to befriend me. What I observed eventhough I was small, I think my cloths I came with and the way the Galadima immediate family and the house helps held me as a very important personality (VIP) visitor and grandson. I enjoyed this vip treatment to the extent that I embraced it. Even to the extent one day in the bus I unwarrantly fought a boy because of a seat he refused to sacrifice for me to sit. Truly the boy was right, and I was on a wrong side. The bus belongs to none of us, therefore, seats are based on first come first serve basis. My father used to buy us new cloths regularly and he made sure that we remain clean I think this culminated in making me clean, smart and attractive especially to the non privileged village boys and girls. That usually wear clean clothes on Fridays because of congregational prayer and ofcourse, during Eids which their parents may be compelled to get them new clothes for the celebration. In my case we got good treatment from our parents by regularly buying new clothes for us.

I visited the junior brother of my grandfather who lived in another village north of Matsai called Kabobi titled Magaji Kabobi by name Malam Yakubu. The people were mainly agrarians and nomadic. Their chief Magaji welded power among the villagers and they liked him. Eventhough, I was small in my longest stayed with him in early 1983, I observed in his courts how he delivered minor judgements of marriages, quarrels about farms, business transaction, inheritance, among others. The difficult ones I know the government in Kaita , Katsina or Kaduna deal with them. The Fulbe of Buluskore, of Kabobi and other nearby villages came to Magaji Kabobi for settlement of disputes.

It is here that I told my second grandfather Magaji that I want hedgehogs many where surprised that I did not mention cow, sheep, guinea fowls, ram, etc but hedgehogs for God sake! Many where surprised even the household members of Magaji were among those amazed with my demand to have the hedgehogs which I hope to take back home when I finish my holidaying in the village. Read my holiday memoirs attentively which I want to share with you.

Hedgehogs are small thorny rodents similar to rats and like porcupines as well. I admired them when I was small and when I grew up. I admired in particular their ways of protecting themselves by coiling in ball like form and exposing their thorns to enemies and their pointed mouths very fascinating also. They are nocturnal creatures that look for foods mostly in the dark while most humans are asleep. I first saw hedgehogs when it was caught in Funtua from farmyard. It was later that I learnt its feeding habits like love for groundnuts, beans and other oily grainy foods. My grandmother Late Hajiya Hauwa stories of our village where we came from turned me to like wilderness, adventure and village life. Her tales influenced me to dare look for hedgehogs and own them as many as I like.

When the opportunity came in 1983 when we closed for the long vacation in September I headed to Matsai although here I was not keen to get the hedgehogs as I did in Kabobi village where I got about five caught by the assistants of my grandfather Magajin Kabobi Yakubu. Life in Kabobi was particularly specially as I got my pets and I crossed on my feet to Niger republic as the village is on the border. With the much effort I was able to made it, I felt contented that when I go back to the boarding house in Government Secondary School, Kagoro I will make a good essay to secure good marks from our mark – stingy English teacher of Form 2F Mr Mahingoda. Things are really changing a man from our village came to Funtua and later my father got him job as a security in one establishment he caught many of these peaceful species – Hedgehogs for me right in Funtua. I must confess now I pity the creatures. I looked at them not as my pets but as another species of creatures that God made to exist on earth and share the eco space with me. Right inside me I admired them and will continue to admired them as rodents that attract my mind.

PART ONE

Funtua Town

Funtua is a settlement which is cosmopolitan exactly it is in the southern part of Katsina state. It was later I came to know about the reasons that brought us to Funtua. My father a staff of Native Authority (NA) Public works, later changed to Local Government was transferred to Funtua as one of the Land officers incharge of survey. Exactly, I was told by my parents I was one year old plus when we came to Funtua. It means that by estimation subjectively we came to Funtua in 1969, that was nine years after Nigerian independence. Nigeria our beloved country obtained her independence in 1960 from the British Colonial Masters. The struggle for independence spearheaded by the nationalists such as late Sir Abubakar Tafawa Balewa, Late Chief Nnamdi Azikiwe, Sir Ahmadu Bello Sardauna. Late Chief Obafemi Awolowo, Late Malam Sa'adu Zungur, Late Malam Aminu Kano and the chunk of masses from the Southern and Northern protectorates and Lagos colony, who lost their lives in the struggle, while others were imprisoned and maimed for the sake of their freedom which we enjoyed today. A popular praise for the town goes like this:

Funtua huntun dutse

Tamagiji mai hayakin kudi

Literally it can be translated as:

Funtua a town with naked mountain

A town govern by Magaji,

with means where one can make money

By all standards Funtua is a town with good hospital, schools, Cooperative shop, markets, motor parks, filling stations, hotels, motels, inns, brothels, electricity, water, good roads, railway station, ginneries, other companies, police station, reading room and other social and economic amenities that promote wellbeing. It is cosmopolitan town with predominant Hausa and Fulani tribes, Yoruba tribe, Igbo, Igala, Nupe, Igbira, Idoma, Tiv, Gbyagi, Kaje and other tribes from the different location of Nigeria. The quarters in the town are well arranged with wider roads that enable ventilation for the residents. Moreover, except for the older settlement quarters such as part of Tudunmahauta, tsohuwar kasuwa and some part of Gangaren Ammani where the roads were narrowed and the arrangement of the houses were not well planned by the urban development officers incharge.

I was following my brothers to Tsangaya school where we learn to memeorise the chapters of Holy Qur'an. My brothers were already ahead of me since they were already grown up that time Isma'il was in primary four, while my cousin Abdulazeez was in class three and Salisu was in two. Our senior sister was about to graduate from the Primary school and was ahead of all of us in both the schools. I learnt she was hoping to go to Girls' College and be educated well our father wants her to leave western education from the primary level. Fortunately for her she was able to outsmart our father and pursued her educational career in Girls College in Kaduna and Later Government Girls' College Malumfashi. Infact she read upto a Postgraduate level. It was a herculean task for her, because girl child education in our area is still facing challenge and is therefore not given much priority. Most parents prefer their female children to marry early. There are many reasons – chiefs are economic status of parents, advice from some Islamic scholars, levels of parents' education, lack of available employments, waywardness of some girls that go to formal schools, difficult of getting husbands when the female children graduate.

In this Tsangaya school headed by Alaramma Muhammadu, nicknamed Maitsagewa I was only memorizing the shorter parts of Holy Qur'an from Chapters Fatiha (Opening chapter of the Qur'an) to Fil (elephant) to. Later I was introduced to writing when my father was asked to buy a slate for me. In the slate the senior students wrote some major letters of Arabic for me, mainly-

A	U	W	Z	B	L	M	Sh	T	N
R	J	M							
B	I	S	M	L	L	R	A	M	A
R	H	M							

Table 1: Some Arabic letters I began with in the Tsangaya

Literally, the letters can be translated as – I seek refuge in the name of God from the Devil an accursed one; In the name of God the beneficent the merciful. When a student memorizes this he will ask to proceed to writing the shorter chapters of Qur'an and the journey continues. This arrangement of study is based on the twenty eight (28) Arabic letters. We were urged to know them and how to read them with vowels such as: short vowels *a. i, u*, long vowels: *a, i , u* and nunnation: *an, in and un*. This will help to make students read the holy Qur'an with ease and how it is supposed to be read.

I enjoyed Thursdays and Fridays as these days no school going, I stayed and played with my friends: Isa, Lawal, Mamuda among others as they too were my age mates not yet enrolled into Primary school. I like the holidays since atleast I was speared the whips and shouts of the senior students in Tsangaya school. One female beggar staying near our house on the road to matoya also restricted my movement. I was naturally afraid of the beggar likely because of her limp nature and her staying on the road side begging. The beggar surprised me one day as she came to greet my mother. I hid in the room to avoid contact with her. She really checked me from going anywhere I like as a boy.

My father's place of work Department of Public Works (Yadi) was in a far area of the town along Zaria road adjacent to Zonal office of North Central State Ministry of Works and opposite the only boarding Boys' Secondary School in the town. He was popular and had many friends, he rode on his big bicycle to office every day except on weekdays when there was no work. He was very dedicated surveyor and land administrator. I later learnt from him he learned survey work from the white men before independence and after independence.

New House 1975

Around 1975 ending we parked to our new house solely built by my father along Zaria road very close to his place of work. In the beginning the quarters where we parked into now was called Sabon fegi. The house was divided into four sections. The main section is the one occupied by my father and our mothers. The house was a mud house well constructed and well planned by the builder and my father because of his nature of his work as a land officer, I think. The second section for our grandmother where I stayed. The third segments for the uncles and the last segment for the guests. The uncles' section belongs to my uncle Umaru Aliyu and his friends.

The new quarters have only few houses and thieves were visiting us luckily enough for us we were lucky, they do not succeed in robbing us or inflicting pain on any one along the quarters as far as I know. My two experience with the thieves that I vividly remembered were while my father had travelled to Kaduna that time he was having a motorcycle CG 175 he left it in our first Zaure since I think he will return the next day or even that day, and the fear of petrol leakage that may be problematic if it happens inside the main house. I was playing with my friends outside the house – Ibrahim and Magaji the thief came and wanted to still the motorcycle he was craftily wanted to send us inside so that he will quickly take the machine and leave while we are inside to avoid our eyes and likely our shouts and report. My mother was in the third zaure she heard us with the stranger who was trying to outsmart us. She called what was happened there. The thief quickly left without succeeding in his evil task. I commended my mother for her onerous job of timely intervention, left to us the thief would have succeeded in sending us by asking us to call someone or get him water from the house. The second thief that I came face to face was a youngman that they chased in the morning hours around 8:00 Pm that he was running helter skeltar to save himself from his pursuers. If they capture him they may lynch him to death. The thief was running helter skeltar to hide. The pursuers were shouting Barawo! Barawo!! Barawo!!! Throwing stones on him and all available objects they came across. I left him passed in front of me I never take even a small stone to stone him. Later one of my friends Lawal accused me of cowardice for not carrying a heavy stone to crush him.

The new house was a duplex the first house was for my father and his two wives as he has his room while the wives have their sitting room and separate rooms. The other house behind was for my grandmother a very influential woman well-travelled, hardworking, industrious, and educated in her own right. Her side mainly divided into two her apartment and that of her guests. When she was asked to leave Saudi Arabia and come back home by my father she accepted and came back to stay with us. In this house there was no well to draw water no pipe borne water we rely on going to Zaria road where there was water sale point and buy from the water Board salesman and bring home. It was during Late General Murtala Ramat Mohammed former Head of State that we were able to get connected to main pipe and water flowed we really celebrated. The leader helped us with his justice, fearness and development. The country was governed well and there were more infrastructural developments all over the country. Infact, it was part of it that water supply was improved. No electricity yet as the main electricity poles were not pegged. Still we enjoyed our lives as we used kerosene lamps, candles and aci balbal. In this house I played extensively with my friends such as Magaji, Yusufu, Ibrahim, Aliyu, Nuhu, Kabir from morning to night time when there was no Tsangaya lessons. I caused serious fire that burnt the hay of Alhaji Mustafa our neighbour and a father of my friend. The hay that time was use for building as they serve as fibre to the soil use to make blocs. I really caused a big lost to his business. Exactly, what happened I carried a match box from the kitchen as we were doing game of hide and seek I wanted to imitate cowboys' film as I lit one dried stalk to enable me see where my friend hide inside the heap of hays as I made my way inside the fire went up. We were even lucky to come out the hays otherwise we would all been burnt inside. My father did not take it easy that very afternoon he gathered all of us – myself, Magaji, Ibrahim and Aliyu he locked his room and whipped us seriously. When the beating was too much for me I hid below his long seat to get relief.

When I reached seven years myself and some of my close friends and neighbours we were taken to Health Department where we were circumcised. I still remember the fear that surrounded my circumcision in particular. Eventhough I am going to eat meat and enjoy myself going nowhere but eat and drink best foods. The persons circumcising cover one with blanket and inject one to reduce the pain. My father played major role in nursing me in order not to scratch the circumcised areas every night I have to sleep in my fathers sitting room where he will use stalked and tighten my legs and hands. Within short time I was healed and became a big boy ready for Primary school. We were proud that we are now almost men will go to school, be with peers and not call mere boys and all sorts of advantages of passing through manhood. I was given gifts of fowls, clothes, money, eggs and many things by neighbours, friends of the family and especially those who wants assistance from my father. Infact how I came to know this is that my father as a public officer serving the local community was not save from the challenges and acute pursue of bribe givers. My father tried to be upright and be a fair officer but these people you can tell about their tactics. I know some gifts were given to me base on the stand of my father not because of my personality, that of my mother or a just charity. Indeed, such are our people even in those days when bribery and corruption were in their buds.

Tsangayar Malam Sa'adu

The school situated along Zaria road, Funtua and adjacent to Baptist priest house. As we came back to Sabonfegi quarters we were enrolled into Malam Sa'adu Tsangaya school because it is closer now to our new home. In this school I came as a transferred pupil already I was attending Malam Muhammadu Maitsagewa school and somewhat now I am advancing. Together with my brothers we were enrolled in this school to continue with our Qur 'anic studies. It is a big school and comprising the small boys the teens and the adult the senior boys referred to as gardawa. The last group are the governors or prefects that oversee us, that belong to the junior class. We suffred their beatings, scolding and teasings, sometimes if Malam Sa'adu was not around some of them bully us to make us fear them. There are main school classes and sometime some of us will be ask to stay and read outside in the open or outside the classrooms.

Since I was not enrolled in primary school therefore whenever I finish my breakfast I will follow my brothers while they will go to the Shehu Primary School, I will go to Tsangaya School they are along the same road, almost stone thrown. I was unlucky in one morning study session that one of the gardawa by name Shu'aibu I fell into his hand that he beat me to the extent that my mother had to rob my body with ointment. Likely, I made noise, or refuse to read the way he wants it or likely I was unlucky that day. My father never complain to the school authority and they never stop me from coming to the school. Rather it was taken as part of training and orientation. Infact, the matter is beyond me left to me I will have protest by not coming to the that school again.

Our group leader our most senior brother Abdu leading us to the school, farms and other chores whenever he choosed to steered us away from the night school I was happy. My view of the school changed after the hard beating from Shu'aibu. Rather than go to the school in most nights to read we will go to Engineer Sule house and watch television. Sometimes he will lead us to old market where those with hidden coins among us will buy roasted heads of fish and other snacks. We will not return home until to 10:00 pm or their about pretending we have just close from the school. They warned me not to reveal the secret of our truancy.

Sometime we received gifts of biscuits from the Baptists' priest who stayed adjacent to our Tsangaya school. He would not mind no matter our number we the children he will give each one his biscuit. I use to wonder does he has money machine in his house or in his church. We the children he likes us and always like to give us biscuits or sweets. The man was so friendly I even use to wonder does this man ever beat anybody in his life. Malam Sa'adu also I have never seen him beating, abusing or rebuking anybody like the gardawa. The two are special people as I never see them beating or scolding any of us. I used to ponder also, although I do not have answer and never approach any elder in order to resolve the puzzle. I asked why are the gardawa having wicked tendencies just like shadow prefects in secondary schools. I likened it to exuberance of the youths and the mentality of new responsibility of leadership entrusted to them. When I reflected on the activities of school prefects especially the shadow prefects and the activities of gardawa my mind use to skip and become confuse on how they deal with the junior ones.

Gudindi Primary School Funtua

When long vacation ended and therefore schools opened for the first term. My father took me to Gudindi Primary School as a pupil and I was enrolled that day in class one in the year first term of 1976. That day I had new friends such as Nuhu and his sister Mary. They were my special friends because they lived close to my house therefore when school closed we use to go home together. The school was full of dedicated teachers such as Malama Turai, Malama Indo, Mr Kunle, Mr Lawrence, Mr Tinedu from Ghana and our Headmistress (Head teacher) Hajiya Rakiya. Most of us in the junior class we so much like student teachers who came from Women Teachers College Kabomo an outskirts village along Katsina road. The Ladies came as Teaching practice student - teachers to our school we really enjoyed staying with them. Probably because of their ability to bring us close to them and their zeal to teach and drilled us on different types of games and sports during physical exercise (PE). We enjoyed games such as seek and hide, race among others.

In the early days of my primary schooling we were going to school on Saturdays, later during Late Murtala Ramat Mohammed the then head of state the Saturday was removed and added to our weekend holiday. My only worried with the school was I was the only person from our home going to the school. My other senior brothers were attending Shehu Primary school also situated along Zaria road. This may be the reason why I became truant instead of going to my school I will divert to Shehu Primary School were I will stay with one teacher by name Malam Sule Abdu who happen to be from our home town of Katsina and a close family friend. Foolishly, I do not know that he will be reporting me to our father. He did so as one day I was dealt with by my father that I always remember the slap. My punishment came in later days with a dirty slap that I have even seen flash of lighting glaring. My father really knew how to punish, I really suffered that day.

Grandmother and Her Love

I found myself as one of the member of the household of my grandmother paternal side. Infact, I never regret being in her quarters. Staying with grandmother was wonderful as one learns stories, learns wisdom, eat well, and sometimes be protected from beating by bullies and sometimes beating from my father. I learnt to memorize in particular Holy Qur'an chapter Sovereignty (Mulk) as a result of her constant reading and mentioning. I learnt cleanliness fasting and how to look for money and tender animals such as sheep and fowls. As for fasting she will fast for ninety days or more serially. That is, she will fast the months of Rajab, the month of Sha'aban and finally end with Ramadan 30/29 days.

Her tales usually focus on her journey by foot, lorries and ship to Mecca. Similarly, she will tell us about our village "Matsai" where she stayed with our grandfather Late Shantali Sani. Whenever, there was no Tsangaya lessons like Thursdays, Fridays, Tashe and Eids festivals myself my cousin sister Assibi and sometime the children from the neighbourhood will joined us to listen to her stories in her sitting room. She told us about the major stream and ponds of Matsai to the extend at that time fishing was serious business was therefore carried out professionally. During one of the fishing time her brother by name Sani was given full basket of fish by her husband to take home. One wonder why water table is now far – far in the water table of this village. Is it burning and engulfed by fire underground. Moreover, still one may wonder where the water went? One can only see the sign like the pits, the stream paths and the sand just like you see in Lake Chad and Ocean in Lagos side in the River side in Onitsha city and similar places. Oh God ! Give us water and revive our land to be fruitful and watery. I learned to memorize many parts of Qur'an because of her constant reciting of some of these chapters. Surprisingly, she too learned it from her new husband Malam in Wagini village. Similarly, her craft like nature of storytelling I also managed to tapped a little.

Tsangayar Malam Umaru

The two brothers jointly managed the Tsangaya, but my teacher was malam Umaru very hard working and he tolerate our behaviours most time. His senior brother Malam Garba also is a Malam and they all have permanent almajirai. When our father made a decision to enrolled us to this new school we were all happy especially my humble self because I left gardawa and their constant beating. Secondly, this new school was just behind our resident, therefore it was near. Malam sometimes beat us mildly as a punishment. In this school like the former it was coeducational. Unfortunately, for our senior ones they were not happy as we came to this school because there will be constant supervision by our father and we were sure he will be coming knowing his nature of loving education and his dislike of truancy.

We were spreading our mats and old cartons on the ground that has no cement or tiles. The regular almajirai who slept in the zaure cum school I wondered how they manage to tolerate the maggots that usually come out from the soil to bite us. In this school after I memorize the lower part of Qur'an I got my new slate that I will start writing chapters of a Qur'an to memorize on it. The tradition is that when you write you take it to the Malam to recite it after you go and drill yourself you come back to the Malam and give him your slate to read off head. When you defend well then you proceed to the next chapter. One chapter that I faced difficulty in committing it to memory was *The Unbeliever* because of the similarities of the verses. I remain committed so that I should not be left by my peers. As I was committed to the boarding school my keen interest in the Tsangaya school reduced my father was disappointed.

An Islamiyya school was established for many of us in the quarters this type of school emphasized knowledge of exegesis, interpretation of the Qur'an, the saying of the holy prophet, peace be upon him, the study of Qur'an memorization, the Arabic language and other fields of Islamic education. We were entrusted under the tutelage of Malam Auwal Dabai he is one of the best teachers I ever heard. Surely, you hardly find a person like him. He constantly advised us regarding acquiring knowledge developing good career and being good to oneself and to others. He is patient, amiable, command respect, jovial and wise. He drew us close to him to the extent that we use to eat together with him whatever his wife cooked. According to him as I heard he schooled in the school of one of the famous scholars in Nigeria, the late Sheik Abubakar Mahmud Gumi who worked, lived and died in Kaduna.

The wisdom of this school is to protect us from becoming waywards, know our religion and become responsible. Exactly, those that were not fortunate among us I observed most of them becoming thieves, and committing other crimes that we cannot do. It was here that I realized the significance of knowledge. I struggle to acquire it no matter the challenges. The mentality of being a College student negatively affected me to continue the Islamiyya and acquire more knowledge. As I returned for holiday I started shunning the school rather concentrating on western education.

Matsai

A village in the northern part of Katsina state. The predominant tribes in the village are Hausa people. There are other tribes and nationalities from Niger republic but are not many. From the foregoing I am blending the history of old Matsai and modern Matsai. Presently, it is under Kaita Local Government area. Going to Matsai from Katsina city as you leave Katsina city by about less than hour drive you will be there. It is very close to the border town of Dankama village which bordered Niger republic. An agrarian and nomadic settlement of our people where water is very scarce now. Life is very difficult as water is scarce. Although we have been hearing tale by the older people that in Bakin kasuwa area of Matsai then the major stream of Matsai overflew with water that even fishing activities were being the then practiced and fishes were in abundance. I may not argue with them and I seem to believe with their saying because of the sandy nature of the soil that look like that of water log areas and the long stretch of pit that look like water ways. A popular song in praise of Matsai is a follow:

Matsai garin Damau

Shakushen mutan 'Yendaki

Literally can be translated as:

Matsai the town of Damau

the envy of 'Yendaki people

From the above song we can deduce that the village was once in its peak and flourishing stage. Looking at the verses again an envy is geared toward somebody or something that is advancing or flourishing. No doubt Matsai without any contradiction was once great and a place to worth living.

The person who brought me all the way from Funtua for my long vacation holidays was Late Alhaji Gimba my step grandfather marrying one of my grandmothers. I enjoyed the journey because before reaching Matsai enroute we went to Danmusa also a district in Katsina state. It was in Danmusa I have seen pictures placed in many public places degenerating the Izala Islamic sect. The picture depicted an Izala sect follower being punished in a grave by an angel. Quickly, I questioned the picture and the makers of it how on earth they went to heaven to snap the picture and bring it back to the world. I wondered as they say little knowledge is dangerous. The purpose was to warn people following the sect of Wahhabism as supported by Saudi Arabia. The pre dominant tribes here are Hausa and Fulani. I was not verse enough in Islamic knowledge but as I had seen the pictures in market and motor park, I concluded that some scholars are wicked they capitalize on the ignorance of others to continue exploiting them. All the pictures are hoax.

Our village is vast and the main job of the people is farming with rearing of animal petty and trading Although the farming is mostly done at a subsistence level, still some reserve some for selling to make ends meet. The moment you take – up from Babbar ruga junction along Dankama village road one can see the farms of Matsai spread all over spread like mats. Millets, guinea corns, beans (cowpeas), groundnuts, Yakuwa (hibiscus plant) are the major grains that are cultivated. They get rainfall from late July to October ending usually. The soil ability to hold water is to poor perhaps it can be attributed to heat, sun and the sandunes all over. The first place you meet when you reach Matsai by Babbar ruga axis is the Yara a sort of village square where one goes to shop, eat foods, drink tea, board bus, gossip, give message and receive message.

One important building I deliberately omitted among the major structures along this axis is the only public Primary school of Matsai where most of our brothers and sisters and our kinsmen from neighbouring villages like Radi, 'Yenhoho attend. In our family, I learnt that the colonial masters compelled my Late grandfather Shantali Sani to enrolled his brothers that was how western education was accepted forcefully in our family. It was from the grandmother I learnt that many white men were coming to visit our grandfather and were very friendly with him. What I discovered when I read History of Katsina emirate and Colonial regime during pre – independence our emirate was very loyal to the British colonial government or masters. In the middle 1950s late Sarkin Katsina Muhammadu Dikko son of Durbi Gidado was close to the colonialists. Infact, it was narrated by many famous Historians that his closeness, relations and loyalty to the British colonial masters earned him the title of Sarkin Katsina. This I can conclude what made every peripheral leader in the whole Katsina province to follow white men otherwise one should bear the consequences of rebellion. One of the consequences is to be deposed and likely imprison or taken to other town such as Lokoja. The colonial masters are interested in politics, economic, and social aspects of our people.

Economically, they collected taxes which they used to run the Native Governments. Similarly, not only in Katsina town Matsai had animals, markets and other related products that have economic values. The white men were so meticulous and serious administrators that during that time they fought the issue of desert encroachment with tree planting and famous 'Gawo law'. Upto day the law is observed as it was gazetted. Our main personal compound where Galadima was the leader of the household was in the centre of the village. In the house adjacent to the room of my chief hostess Baba Abu laid my Late grandfather Shantali Sani the senior brother of Galadima Suleiman. That was where they buried him when he died of strange illness that they were not comfortable to reveal to anybody. I learnt that he suffered as he was taken to the only big hospital in Katsina province but alas! Grandfather never recovered from that strange sickness. We have a saying that everyone of us has his way of taking his leave transition to new life. Bye – bye daddy.

Socially, colonial masters were interested in imposing their type of education against our Tsangaya and our trade (vocational education). Theirs is you must go to formal school like – Elementary school, Middle schools, Higher institutions to courses at home and in England. Our early elite served them as clerks and administrative staff mostly. Most of the fight or struggle indulged by our great nationalists was against killing of our blacksmithing, carving trade, weaving trade, goldsmitting, tannery among others, the white left us like orphans. Our technology was destroyed and theirs was promoted. There are some places that we can still clap for them and thank them by eliminating slavery and slave trade. In Matsai the southern part terrain is where is located a heap of large stones and some pieces that are historically important in nature and for us. According to Late Malam Barau Matsai, Hon Urwatu and Late Shantali Abdullahi Lawal as they separately narrated to me. The stones served as sanctuary for the early Matsai settlers against the intruders chiefs were warriors – Kaura Hasau from Maradi in Niger republic, Kaura from Dankama among others. Who left their territories seeking for fortunes such as slaves and other economic items. It was said that one kanya tree in front of the stones and large cave received it share of the pre-colonial time raid adventures as an arrow was seen hooked on it major trunk. As they reaveled to me there is water pond in the cave. It was narrated that the founder of modern Matsai and the first Shantali Late Kane of blessed memory struggled to keep away these warriors away.

Wilderness

I followed Dandare, Tari, Baba Halilu to farms where we rode on donkey back and chased birds. Sometimes I followed Baba Urwatu and others to irrigation areas where they cultivated pepper, tomatoes, garden eggs among others. There are also guava trees. The people are hardworking I even grafted one white guava with the red one to practice what my Integrated science subject teacher taught us in class. The technique they did in the Fadama area was to excavate the sandy soil and will reach water with these shallow wells like pits. They were using the water to water their land through some channels and related techniques. The bush is vast no threat as far as I know and witnessed. We were in the bush to get food for the horse of Galadima. Horses are wonderful animals, they eat and eat, and keep on eating from time to time. That is why they say: to rear horse you must be wealthy. In this village no police or prison yet people were staying peacefully.

What usually the farmers cultivate in their farms are: guinea corn, millet, beans, groundnuts principally. While close to some of the water logged areas and dug wells woodlots trees are reared and planted. These economic threes are farmed and their cultivation is encouraged by the government. Some of these economic trees include: neem tree, turare tree, gum Arabic tree. The European Economic Community (EEC) with conjunction of Kaduna State Government and later Katsina state government encouraged the planting business in this arid zone. The abled young ones, the aged and boys all engaged in different aspects of farming to support their families. I once visited late Shantali Abdu in his tree farm busy working. The beans and groundnuts remnants were used as animal fodders and interestingly they store the stalks of corns and millet on top of trees in the farms and on top of some of the rooms. Economically, some that do not need much of the remnants sale them to those that need much.

Whenever we were in the farms we played more than work. Dandare who was some years ahead of me led us very tolerant and his parent who were said to be in Niger republic did not enroll him in L'ecole like me. He came to Matsai to look for money. We ran and use catapults to attack birds and used stick to attack rats and any rodent that come our way. No elder was nearby to control us we went on playing more than doing what we were therefore send to do. I wondered why we mostly spear bush lizards that are ugly. My search for hedgehogs was still on as I still looked for them under heaps of corn stalks and that of beans parked to dry before transporting or storing them on top of trees. Later I was told to get hedgehog one has to come in the night hours or at dawn. This was quite beyond me, I cannot come and the elders will not even allow me to do the nocturnal visit to the farms at that period. Moreover, tale of Kambulti spirits a sort of cult and other evil creatures that move in the night hours will not allow me to undertake the journey to the bush even if I have cutlass, short stabbing knife and sickle with me. Although, I am a person who does not believe in charms and most of these superstitions but the stories and influence of grandmother made me fear. In most cases, fear retards one struggle to reach his pinnacle. I really believed spirits do exist as I was taught by my religion scholars as culled from chapters in the Holy Qur'an they were notably mentioned as in Chapter Mankind … "From among the jinn and mankind" 114/6 and in the chapter Beneficent "And He created the Jinns from a smokeless flame of fire" (55/15). I put it in my mind that I will get my hedgehogs and God will assist me but how? I do not have idea yet. The opportunity will definitely come will my optimism and struggle.

PART TWO

Marmaru

It is a festivity practice every year after harvest usually around September of every year. The festivity of display of youthfulness, agility and a mini durbar lead by the Matsai youths. People eat and drink and wear new and clean cloths while sports such as wrestling, boxing and display of horse and donkey durbars were engaged especially by the male young adults watched by almost everyone. Infact everyone who cares participate in one way or the other, what I observed during the festivity was the celebrants were mostly the youths. One of my grandfather Malam Barau Matsai, tall very jovial, energetic and one of the most popular politician in Matsai as almost whoever matters when he comes to Matsai must look for him. To coordinate his campaigns, and protect his interest when it comes to voting. He really made a very successful career in village politics. Sometimes even the small boys will go round the village campaigning for him 'Malam Barau Matsai NPN". The boys include one boy from Galadima's compound Known as Arma, you will hear the voices of the boys chanting Malam Barau Matsai NPN. NPN was then the most popular party it won elections in 1979 and 1983 in the country. Whenever the little boys finished campaign they will come waiting for Malam Barau for the usual gifts of coins to buy groundnuts, biscuits and related sweeties. He ushered us into the arena of the wrestling festivity Marmaru free. The mini stadium was a thatched fence square where youths were displaying their prowess by engaging in wrestling, boxing, dance and various kind of sports and competition to celebrate another ongoing Marmaru.

Although, I was not big enough to read things properly at that time, however, I discovered many negative things about the festival as some youths took girls to their rooms for something that can be frowned at. My friend Lawal told me the girls willingly cooked foods and made pepper soups with chicken and bring Fura as well to their fiancés. From these visits other behind the scene flirtings do occurred. Lawal as son of the soil and dweller of Matsai knew better and as they say – monkey resembles man. The way I watched the exuberance of some youths both the boys and the girls they can do anything to enjoy the festival. What I ate that really I enjoyed was cooked meat seasoned with condiments like daddawa, pepper and other local spices.

One popular mad man that always caught our attention as boys was Samama an aged man of probably late 60 years that was always in dirty babbar riga that went from end to end of the village beating and abusing no one. We boys we fear him especially when coming closer to him as he murmured his mouth as if talking with unseen people. Our fear was that of sudden attack because of his madness. His main resting area was the Yara square where good samaritans bought tuwa for him and sometimes remnats of danwake, dambu or tea and bread will be reserved for him to feast on hungrily. Other side attraction of this festival is the durbar organized by the youths and led by the Sarkin Samari who rode on a horse and others rode on different beasts of burden while others followed on their feets singing, praising and merrying. Some of the boys rode on beast of burden such as horses and donkeys while some boys on stalk horses playfully following real horses behind jovially following their brothers. A technician used stalks of corn to make an aeroplane as big as real plane and it was displayed for onlookers to see near yara as the epicenter of the festival. The last but not the list this young technician also established a local radio station that broadcasted within a short band.

My grandmother told me that during the reign of our grandfather there were more festivals that use to attract guests including white men who came to watch some of the events in Matsai like wrestling, boxing, dances and related events. Also prominent among the important personality that visited for the events includes most of the village heads around Matsai such as: Kabobi, Gishirawa, Radi, 'Yenhoho and neighbouring villages of Niger republic. This festival has a long history and is being modernized every year especially as the youths now go out to many cities and are coming back with new ideas. Moreover, religion seriously curtailed some of the unwanted cultures that Marmaru was known with. Girls going to male youths' rooms were prevented from such intermingling that are morally bad. Similarly, some youths still introduced smoking and drinking that are alien to our culture in this part of the world. What I never observed and unable to identify the Kaduna state Government officials or the Katsina Local Government officials presence in the arena of these festival of Marmaru. Presently, Ministry of Information and Culture need to come and participate to promote Marmaru. Likewise, Katsina State, Arts and Culture Bureau need to recognize and identify this festival and classify as part of what tourists are expected to see. It will help to generate revenue for the government and individuals through promoting their wares and services. Our culture and tradition can be portrayed to the world to see and appreciate where it fit them.

Market Day in Matsai

Every Tuesday was marked as a market day where businessmen and buyers come both men and women will come to sale and buy. This day lorries and cars will come from Katsina, Kano, Dankama, Igboland, Yorubaland and other related places in other to purchase grains, animals and other type of wares. At every Tuesday of the week businessmen of different wares come and sale their commodities also buyers that come from different places especially neighbouring places such as Radi, Kagadama, Kaita, Katsina and even other traders from neighbouring states who will come to buy animals, millet, beans, ropes,fans among others. Market day is a happy day for most people, not only the buyers and sellers. It is a day that goods one can select from will be available to purchase, a day that transport is available from early morning to late evening around 9:00 pm local time. Market day to us is like a festival day, the village look beautiful.

The market day afford Matsai people to get lorries, buses and few cars that can risk crossing the sand to Matsai. As of those days it was only on market days in particular Tuesdays for Matsai and Mondays for Kagadama that vehicles for transport would be available. I entered the market and sightseeing from group to group appreciating different kind of wears such as foods, utensils, animals, barbecued meats of small and big animals, ropes, clothes, shoes, drugs, etc. On market days' women preferred fura/hura, kosai, kuli- kuli, waina, tuwo, danwake, dambu, etc for sale. This help them to get revenue. While those who fetched water also engage in their business. It was in the market I saw a technique of cooling soft drink through putting the soft drink bottles inside a pot with clean water inside.

On the side of the Government I observed lack of recognition as there was no any erected shop built by her, or supporting the traders to do so. The Local Government in Katsina is its responsibility since they know how to generate revenue and impose payments of certain amounts that it sent her agents to collect. I therefore, imagined the neglect. Late Shantali Abdullahi Lawal narrated to me since the pre independence at the time of colonial masters traders were paying revenue to the government collected by the Native Authority (NA) and the Village heads officials. He emphatically informed me coming to Matsai market as of then a trader will be compelled to pay the stated amount as sale tax. There was also purchase tax as of then being accrued to the coppers of Government as revenue. As narrated by this leader and affirmed by him the activities of 'Yentare that intercepted the traders from Faranshi and other neighbouring places amalgamated in working to curtail the popularity and breadth of Matsai market. They were saboteurs to the market and to the government as well. As later I was told they will say: Are you ready to sale? If you reach Matsai you will be compelled to pay sale tax". On my subsequent visit to Matsai in the late 1990s the Matsai market was no more as Kagadama market, Dankama market Kaita market within the vicinity sprouted up interestingly and the traders, the buyers and the rest of the people focused on these newly flourishing markets that were categorically boast on: Mondays, Wednesdays and Fridays.

PART THREE

Going to Kabobi

I was so happy as Galadima my grandfather billed me to go and visit his brother at Kabobi and spend some days of my holidays with Magaji Malam Yakubu. I was so happy as I will be on the wild there also. Fortunately, enough for me and unknown to me it was here that my hedgehogs gathered to be parked waiting for me to come. I really seized the opportunity. It was part of our tradition when you visit your relatives you will be ask to visit all the recognized relations far and near to greet them. This was the cause of my sojourn to Kabobi, perhaps my first visit to this part of our land. My chief host in Kabobi I knew him very well since he came to Funtua for naming ceremonies of my junior sisters and brothers and when my beloved mother died in 1981 he also came therefore we knew each other to some extent. The only strangers to me are his family members, the land and my new friends chief of which were Rabi'u and Abdullahi. Rabi'u in particular was more close and always available to play with and we went for sightseeing and errands together. The friends of your friends are automatically your friends. This opportunity to have more friends, notwithstanding I was steered by my grandfather to stay more at home than follow friends anyhow. I do not mind much for the restriction of especially staying at home as our father has been restricting me from going anywhere also back in Funtua.

Kabobi is what you will describe as boosting land with its businesses, farming and I suspect petty smuggling activities by miscreants in clothes, drugs, foods and related wares and rearing of animals mostly sheeps and goats. Already I learnt some of the songs the singers sang for my host like:

"*Magaji Kabobi, zare yakare*

Illo yacinyemana kada".

Literally, translated as:

Magaji Kabobi the thread finished

Illo had exhausted our cotton.

This is only part of the song it is a long song, with the chorus: "Illo yacinyemana kada". This is the only part that I can remember now.

Most probably they were from Niger republic because of the use of the name 'Illo' I was unable to see them when later I reached the land and unable to ask my brothers that visited the land before me. Magaji was lively, charming, easy going, and had the habit of true big men of giving gifts. He was indeed very friendly he will not mind hosting me and my friend for a long time chatting and laughing with us. Most cases that he resolved in his courts or chamber are on marriages, trusts, inheritance, properties, among others he gave good verdicts and in my presence no one will dare ask me to leave the court where the cases were usually decided. The court's sessions held in his court attached to his house and when he went to inspect property or attend meeting while it happened I was at home I will stayed in the court to rest but not climbing his office chair, I never tried that. What shaped my life was my father as he taught us manners to respect elders and one should be where God place him. My father was a typical moralist and Hausa man, a father that was attached to his tradition culture and discipline. If my father was sitting, we cannot pass him with our shoes on our feets we must remove them as a sign of respect. Although, this act of removing shoes is practiced in almost all Hausa/Fulani compounds. In addition, in the boarding school where I schooled we were taught to respect our seniors. Exactly in the boarding house our dining halls where we received our meals were segregated. The first one for the senior students - form four and the final year students (form five), we the junior ones forms one to three we had ours adjacent to the senior students' hall. What I do not know is that whether their ratio as senior were slightly better than ours. This taught me people are not equal as we are, some are more honoured than others. While going to class from the hostels we the junior students had our separate paths and the big boys (the senior) had theirs. If one mistakenly or deliberately followed their ways, he will be punished with one of the capital punishment.

Earlier in the day Galadima as he asked Baba Halilu to take me to Kagadama to hand me over to his junior brother who will be in the market as usual to deliberate on cases and other matters that were usually brought to him by his subjects. After bidding goodbye to my hostess my grandmother Baba Abu full name Zainab, she was the senior wife among my grandfather Galadima three wives. It was the tradition of our people the senior wives are leaders in most households when I reached the house Galadima asked me to be accommodated there. Sometimes I slept in her rooms but later when I had friends Galadima gave me a room by the main house entry well roofed with a hay thatched. The first room to reach through the main gate of his wing of the compound my friends left their houses after informing their parents to come and stay with me.

As motor came and we boarded it to Kagadama market where we will meet Magaji Yakubu as is their tradition that every market day they will come and attend to the administration of the market and land. I conservatively estimated we spend less than an hour in the motor that penetrated sand dunes and was jam packed, the kilometres we covered were either five or six. The sluggishness of the journey was cause by the bad condition of the road. The roots of shrubs and sand making the old range rover sluggish and the commotion in the motor disturbing the driver. Range rovers, land rovers, tractors enjoy this type of roads than fords, Peugeot or any motor. Even these desert prone motors sometimes find it difficult to penetrate the sand and speed as needed.

Kagadama Market 1983

Enroute to Kabobi village Baba Halilu the junior brother of my father who was asked to escort me to Kabobi was directed to take me and hand me over to Magaji who was at the market. That was how I had to be in the market in his court in that Monday. I was immediately given sit to sit down and take a rest. As his guest and visiting grandson I started receiving meat, fura, water, and different kind of foods that I care to eat or drink and that are worth taken to an august visitor. I ate and drank fura till I satisfied without any pullako or self deprivation due to shyness or nostalgia. I met him with people that I thought were discussing sensitive issues that affect people. Not necessary dispute as I observed the people that we met with him.

In this market the Katsina Local Government had did the needful by building stalls and were well organized eventhough no provision for locking at the end of market day. The shops were open but had the shade to protect the owners from sun and rain. The Katsina Local Government realized the value of the market therefore made the building and were generating revenue. There was only abattoir where animals were checked and slaughtered hygienically. Late Shantali Abdullahi Lawal stated to me that Kagadama market came into existence as result of the activities of interceptors who met traders that came from different direction to sale their wares. According to him even the market got it name from this event that is, 'Kagadama' that is 'if you like'. Meaning if you like to sale and save yourself the burden of tax paying when he reaches Matsai. One should sale to them and refuse to go to the formal market in Matsai where he will pay sale tax. Most people according to the legend they cooperated by selling their wares to these saboteurs. Later the colonialist/NA approved for the establishment of Kagadama market and entrusted it to Magaji Kabobi Yakubu.

The market was well arranged with section of animal sellers in the extreme end north west axis, the utensils sellers at the centres, near them are provision such as flours, sugar, biscuits sellers staying close to them. Foods such as grains, cooked foods have their sections as well. There was almost everything in this market as sellars and buys brought wares from Katsina, Kano, Igboland, Yorubaland and neighbouring Niger republic. The market starts from Sunday, that is, a day to the actual market day. It was a big market indeed and it was able to bring people from different areas of that country specifically to buy cattle, small animals, camels, donkeys, fowls, grains such as beans and millet.

By evening time, the market started to coil back as buyers and sellers started to pack for their different destinations. I was asked to get ready so that we can walk home to Kabobi. My escort had already left and probably had returned to Matsai.

Walking to Kabobi

No motor to climb or bike to ride except some beast of burden like horses and donkeys. In our case we walked to the village talking and exchanging pleasantries with those we met passing us. I can conservatively measure the distance walking to be around 40 minutes walk by an average walker. Not that we refused to board a motor to Kabobi, because non followed toward Kabobi village rather the went back to their various destinations such as Kaita, Katsina, Niger republic, Kano, among others.

As I trekked I don't mind, I like walk. In the bush while in keeping with my dream of getting hedgehogs I started to think I may see it crossing the road so that I can run to carry it as it may coil back. We started to see some outskirts houses of Kabobi, later the propeller of water point can be seen from where we were. The journey shortened and ended by the time we reached home.

We reached Kabobi around the dusk prayer time in company of Magaji Kabobi and his council with few aides. Immediately he handed me to the senior wives who was to be my chief hostess and see that I stayed safe during my visit. By coincidence in this household like that of Galadima in Matsai there were three wives. The wives of my grandfather were friendly and accommodative I related with them well. The senior wife was taken care of my needs in the house like food, my place of rest, my baths and other needs.

Dalha was a trusted aide to Magaji Yakubu he stayed with his family in the vast compound of Magaji Kabobi. He attended to many of Magaji's needs, he travelled to do many chores of his master. This man probably a Fulani was a confidential secretary to Magaji, ADC, house help and messenger as well. He was easy going person that I found also easy to befriend as well. Sometimes I followed him to the water point of the village where he worked as the operator and he served with dedication. The animals will come and drink and people will also fetch the water and carry to their homes. The Government established the water point to encourage rearing of animals and for the provision of clean water to its citizens wherever they are. My young mind planned for me to visit all the farms I was passing. There were many farms surrounding Kabobi like ring. How to execute my mission of getting my heart desire and my pet I did not finalize. Deep inside my heart I knew God will help me to succeed. We walked peacefully in the bush, no expecting attack or any inconvenience. Rural areas have a particular mood of peace and tranquility compare to urban areas where you cannot confidently walk without attack or seeing something that will provoke you. Imagine walking a distance of 40 minutes with dignity without pick – pockets, car horns, bike attack as it wants to share road with you. No hazard of industrial smoke of any nature. One can only hear birds and other species of animals making touching songs, crying and complaining that we cannot interpret correctly but we listened to some we enjoyed, some touched us deeply inside as they remind us of life and it challenges.

Kabobi Village

I now became familiar with Kabobi village. I can go anywhere I like but with some restrictions as any move that I made I will be reported to Magaji as their leader they like to see to my safety. Unlike Matsai where I can determine my time to leave home and time to return, here it was different eyes were really on me likely because of my safety. Therefore, my chief host and his wives observed me together with Dalha his close aide. What fascinated me much was that even my friends they had to screen them. I later found out that they knew their parents. Therefore, their ability to know every family very well determine who I will be allow to play with and move with in the village. Like my father he always warned me on types of friends the I should have. As far as night life was concern I do not know anything as I cannot go anywhere here. Do they have witches? Do they have Shafi mulera? Do they have many evils in the night? There were certain things that were beyond my comprehension? Although, as of then I never care to inquire or to insist in knowing as Magaji said so and be it, therefore, I was restricted and I obeyed. Later during our play as we were discussing Rabi'u told me that as he was send on an errand one night he saw some figures in complete white dresses with no heads when he reached home he felt really sick and his parents had to sought for the assistance of Malam to pray for him before he recovered. Rabi'u's family house was in the eastern side of Kabobi village. Do they have these spirits abundant in this land, I queried myself? Or are their many cult activities perpetrated by the magicians? The questions that I never find their answers even when later I grew up.

I spent my nights with the members of the households where we usually gather in the senior wive room to listen to stories and they will ask me about Funtua, my parents and my boarding school in Kagoro. I am familiar with them therefore we will go on talking until sleep defeat me and my mat with blanket will be ready for me to call it a day. I enjoy my sleep in the rooms that were secured with locks. In the night I hardly come out to go to the toilet because I hate darkness therefore I will not drink much water or drink fura in the night to cause me going to toilet.

As I stated earlier the whole of Kabobi was surrounded with farms, where beans, groundnuts, millet, guinea corn, some vegetables were cultivated such as jute, hibiscus plant. There were some roads but narrow that will led one to Niger republic. I became a bush boy as already I loved life in the wild. I once trekked and crossed the border and inside myself I felt satisfied that atleast I cannot easily get visa to cross to another country let me freely cross to Niger republic without any visa or challenge from Immigration officers. I learnt that one of my friend's father was a chronic drinker, I will not reveal him to avoid embarrassing myself and his person. Even then I wondered where were they cooking the burukutu, where were they brewing it and where were they drinking it. Do they have night bars or brothels in Kabobi? They must have a house where men relax and pastime. Is this the reason why my grandfather prevented me going out in the night? Wherever, you have drinking joints like burkutu bars there must be free women and gambling as well. God Has His congression and Devil has his. Ofcourse, not all men are good there must be wayward people. In our society to drink alcohol is a sin and it is completely abhorred. A drunkard is seen in the society as a hopeless man.

Water in Kabobi was not difficult to obtain as in Matsai, I have been to a well close to Magaji's house and it was filled with water. Infact no much suffering for water here. The trees were few in the village and were mostly palm trees such as goriba, giginya, and dogon yaro (bedi) and some shrubs such as Kaba, Kalgo, sabara among others. There are also fruits and economic trees such as: Kanya, magarya, kurna. Economically, most of these resources are used as foods, raw materials and as shade against the piercing sun of the sahara. Kanya is a fruit tree that is eating when it small ball like fruits mature. It is dried when it is in excess to preserve. It is sold all over the country especially where Hausa people reside. Likely, magarya produce fruits that are used for normal drink and medicinal purposes and it leaves are used to wash the death. The villagers used to sale it and get cash. Kaba is used to make mats, ropes, hats, fans, adaka, etc. The entrepreneurs (makers) sale the manufactured goods to wholesalers who also sale in cities especial hotels where tourist purchase.

Sometimes I stayed in the court of Magaji conversing with him. His radio always when he was on seat in the court if there were no administrative issues to attend he will open his radio for us to listen to news, religious programmes, drama, some relevant music and discussion programmes. There was no television or any viewing centre in the village no library or news stand to get information. Therefore, the radio of Magaji linked us to the outside world. Infact, we were lucky ones then. In a typical village environment like this it is not surprising. Magaji was an epitome of authority- he represent the Governor, represents the Chairman of the local Government, he represents the District head of Kaita (Sarkin Sullabawa) he represents the Commissioner of police, he represents the chief judge. In short, Magaji is a government as he rules, judges and decides with her consent. What surprised and puzzle me much he had not been to the Faculty of Law Zaria or Faculty of Administration all in Ahmadu Bello University Zaria or similar Law Faculties in University of London, University of Ibadan or even Oxford university. I cannot remember ever seen any book in his house that he may refer to in his judgements.

Cattle Dungs

The wives of Magaji Kabobi were good cooks, I like their ways of cooking they will make sure that beans cooked well and the fura they pounded was good to drink and very palatable. For these and many more I regarded them with respect and ready to take their orders. One evening the wife on duty wanted to cook wasa – wasa which was usually made from beans when pounded a bit it is like a couscous or cooker oats. Without repeating there were few trees in Kabobi upon all the tree planting exercises practised every blessed year in the state. Sometimes firewood was not as available as the villagers need. Here kerosene stove was not common. The kerosene they used mostly for those that afford to have kerosene lamps. As a result of the food for our dinner we were asked together with my friends to go and pick cow dungs to use as firewood to cook for us, I wondered how on earth cattle dungs can be converted into firewood and get fire to cook our dinner. Another thing I observed and discovered the cattle dungs were used for is pasting it on woven basket to make it strong and lasting. Sometimes if you observe woven basket carried these dungs. Perhaps the dungs may be an insect repeller to prevent termites from eating up the woven basket. Back in Funtua my father as a farmer use to take me to farm, I also discovered that cattle dungs were use as organic fertilizer for plants to sprout better.

In the open at the eastward axis of the village we followed the path of the cattle where they followed going west or going eastside, either way they move as well as excrete picking anything eatable and drinkable. They followed the labi to reach Kaduna, to Plateau state, Benue state, to Kogi state, to Niger state, to Imo state to Lagos to neighbouring countries such as Benin republic, Cameroun, part of Ghana, among others looking for animal pastures. We picked the dried dungs and put on a bowel we went with. Surprisingly, under some dungs we saw different creatures such as black ants, and different kind of ants that I never see. I hope I will see hedgehogs with its children taking cover below the dung or beside it. The cattle as they pass either from the east or from the west they excrete which will quickly dry on the sand of the sahara desert that quickly consumes the watery particles. It is only the dried dungs that are pick for the fire to easily catch and be useful for cooking. In the open we played and discussed our affairs of teenagers.

We returned home and no detergent to wash my hand as I used to clean my hands in Funtua. Therefore, I do not mind much since I used left hand in picking the dungs. My other friends they do not mind to pick with the right or wash their hands as we return. I thank my mother that I lost to a sickness in 1981 when I was in class six about to pass out from Gudindi primary school she taught me hygiene habits. No matter what, before eating tuwo or eating anything with my hands directly I must wash them, it was a golden rule. She supervised me seriously as far as my training was concern. I followed her teaching even after her demise.

Journey to Buluskore

Buluskore is a predominant Fulani community under Kabobi. As we paid a visit to the village while they were marking a day probably sharo festival where I followed as part of entourage of Magaji Kabobi. We set off around 10: 00 am local time to me hoping to discover new land and to see new people. To Magaji and his staff to undertake usual routine job they have been doing and doing for years. We trekked to the village and I estimated that we walked for nearly less than an hour, it may be less than fourty minutes. As I looked at the way we were moving with Magaji his walking and his tradition of asking after his people along the road cause the delay in reaching Buluskore; You know Fulbe greeting is not brisk but comprehensive:

'Yallabai, barka da zuwa;

Yaya iyali;

Yaya jama'a;

Yaya shekara?

Sometimes even animals would be asked after. Literally, the above greeting can be translated as follows:

Sir, you are welcome;

How are your family?

How are your people?

How is the time, sir?

As we reached the village/settlement, immediately we went to the stand or mobile court of Magaji Kabobi. As we settled and rest for some minutes people started to troop to the court for greetings and the business of the day. In my mind I kept on wondering what a wonderful God, that created many people and spread all over the earth. I never been here so for all these years these people are here living. I queried, is our President Alhaji Shehu Shagari knows about them? How about Alhaji Lawal Kaita the Governor of Kaduna state does he knows about them?

The sharo itself was not merely a pastime far say but a culture. I in particular detested it and even the government in most cases frowned at it. I learnt that in other places they banned it. Sharo a culture of Fulani people that was done yearly by abled yougmen where pairs will each beat each other with different types of whips or sticks. The essence is to show prowess, agility, promise and masculity. Above all whoever, did not cry atleast will get a wife and is a proud to his clan. One song that attract me was the children welcoming camels crossing-

Rakumi! Rakumi!! Zololo

Maida gabanka zuwa Agadas

Agadas ta tafi tabarka

Meaning:

Camel! Camel!!Very long

Concentrate on your journey to Agadas

Agadas is far from you

Whoever composed this song, that children were singing for the camel used his brain intelligently. He was able describe the long nature of camel, extremely long creature (Zololo). Secondly, Agadas city in Niger republic is well known with its camels, as the tuaregs businessmen brings potash, salts, date palm fruits, etc they follow trans Saharan routes back to Agadas to prefer for yet another journey back. Now the camel owner focus is reaching Agadas eventhough it is far

The answer to my file of questions was answered immediately as I realized that Magaji has no time for pastime or joke always engage as he was their Local Government Chairman, their Governor and their President as he represented these leaders. Line up of deliberations and cases here was execution of cases and referring serious criminal cases to Alkali courts in Katsina. Some couples came regarding marriage issues, some came regarding wealth (cattle). Some came to complain of tyranny meted to them. While others came complaining to Magaji about animals eating their grains. Most of the cases were on interactions among men and women. Inheritance issues were not seriously treated as this issues need deep knowledge. Although at that time I do not know Islamic law of inheritance but I also knew that Magaji cannot delve into it without consulting his chief Imam and other Islamic scholars in his council/courts. The implication is that if a leader judges wrongly and the inheritors report to the Chief judge serious problem may arise which will lead to imprisonment or deposition of an office holder by the Government.

During launch period after we said our early afternoon prayer (Az - zuhur) Magaji order for launch we ate barbecued meat and followed with fura. I ate and drank to my fill, this will enable me to forget other foods such as kosai, waina, tuwa, dan – wake, dambu, nono and some that I do not know atoll. My nature is when I get meat and Fura they replace tuwo king of foods for me. When my stomach was filled I walked around to see happening in the market like festival area and inhale breath of fresh air. The placet was not as big as others that I visited previously but it was well arranged and secured. The Ardo and his lieutenants and above all Magaji Kabobi were on top of the situation. I saw Fulani with their calabashes of nono well dressed and decorated faces with powder and black pencil like colour. The men were holding sticks and swords. Some brought sticks to sale, some brought sheep and so on. I observed everyone that came to the arena with one mission or the other. Some girls brought waina to sale, while others were selling breads on trays. Donkeys, bicycles and horses were also available parked aside waiting for the owners.

Many of the guests and Ardo that came to greet Magaji were asking of me, and Magaji was proudly telling them I am his grandson on holiday from Funtua. I got gifts that some were not place on my hands but on the aides who never bring to our household or to Magaji in particular. I respected the people because of their resilience to stay where God placed them and even their death parents. Really there were no electricity, no pipe borne water, no even basic clinic nearby, no school for their children, no police station, no telephone, no post office, no courts, no library, no tarred roads, no television to watch. The negative list is long. Yet these people in this part of Nigeria occupying a small area were happy in their own ways. These people predominantly nomadic are hardworking but neglected, they reared animals bigger and small.

When evening approached Magaji Kabobi started to conclude major and minor cases after investigations and calling witnesses to testify. Women were sometimes call but they stayed afar behind men and were asked to state their opinions regarding marriages, divorces, inheritances and related matters. We reached home safely around 6 :30 pm local time, we were welcomed back

We have Ministry of Education in the Sates and Federal levels, yet the development of establishing schools for the nomads had not yet reach these people and their village. The people need it to become more civilize in new world order. I have seen young beautiful Fulani girls and agile Fulani boys that supposed to be in school like me instead they were not going, but following cattle and some therefore behaving like cattle especially when provoke. The politicians and civil servants that are in charge of certain establishments and policies shunning to educate these people are not helping matters as refusing education and social facilities will never augur well for us. When they start to ask their share from society in general they may cause riot, block our roads, stop us from going to our farms and gardens. The government and the society for long have been ignoring these people and are taking it lightly. They move with sticks, with swords, catapults and short stabbing knives. In comparison to most of us they know bushes and thick forest areas across Nigeria and the land of neighbours like Cameroun, Benin republic, Niger republic, Chad republic, Ghana, Mali among others.

PART FOUR

Visit to Dankama

I stayed for some days now, almost six days exactly as another market day is coming just a day away. Magaji had a daughter in faraway village of Dankama under the leadership of Sarkin Fulani. In this village Magaji's daughter Rabi was married to Sarkin Fulani the village head of Dankama as a result he was making plan to sent me to her to greet her and stay for some days with the family. I like the idea and I appreciate the plan, I will go and visit my aunt and see yet another world that I have never been. It is also a border town closer to the Niger republic. It has a popular market very boastful market and well known. In addition, the town entirely was an open gateway to some of the professional and amateur smugglers. This in particular assisted in making the village above it peers like Matsai, Girka, 'Yan'daki. The market day is Wednesday. Every Wednesday from far and near traders, buyers and officials visit the market. Some are coming from Katsina, Batsari, Jibiya, Kano, Niger republic, Southern Nigeria, Eastern Nigeria and other near and closer vilages and towns in the North.

Who was this Gwoggo Rabi, wife of Sarkin Fulani? She was the only daughter of Magaji and she had only one brother. A beautiful and friendly middle aged woman. They were only two both to their mother and to their father Magaji Kabobi. I learnt that Magaji never had any child beside these two. I have never seen her before in my life when I was asked to be escorted by Dalha to go and visit her I wondered we never see each other. What can I do, after all I will still see more parts of my country and our people? As Dalha reached Dankama with me. We went on market day in order to get motor which fly the road abundantly on market day. These motors include range rovers, land rovers, tractors, land cruisers, and worn out hiece buses among others. We boarded a land rover that penetrated the sand and took us to Dankama with some delay as sometime sandunes had to cause commotion on the major roads leading to Dankama.

Dalha will leave me, as he was instructed. Gwoggo I learnt that she was black in complexion, charming and friendly like her father Magaji. Really I found this story about her truth. She welcomed us happily the other wives of Sarki came to her room to welcome us. Her stepson by name Bashir also welcomed us to the house. Sarki also welcome us and asked about his inlaw and other relations. As later I was told Sarki and Magaji are closed relations. Dalha bid us goodbye and left to attend to some needs in the market before leaving for Kabobi. Gwoggo Rabi asked me to feel at home she brought me fura and food to drink and eat. The house is bigger than that of Magaji and here they are wealthier perhaps due to the businesses they may be engaging and their ability to get more revenue for the palace or courts of Sarkin

Fulani. In most cases myself and my new friend the stepson of Gwoggo Rabi we stayed in the court to listen and watch proceeding in the palace of the Sarkin Fulani. One event that I easily remember was in one of morning session in the court one man fell down and was writhing in pain. We were told he was seized by the spirits, actually he was just epileptic. Later the place he was seized was burned. I wondered is this scientific or superstition?

Bashir my friend was the son of Sarkin Fulani I was about five years older than him. He was very accommodative we played together and slept together in Gwoggo's room. I learnt that one of the wife of Sarki was his mother but because of good courtesy nature of our people and to promote good living and harmony Bashir was giving to my Gwoggo. It was to comfort Gwoggo as she never had her own child. We entered town and usually on special errands by the wives. The house was big enough for our plays and rest. Like Kabobi night life was not our business, therefore, I do not know Dankama in the night, as I do not know Kabobi in the night. I observed Sarki do not go anywhere in the night he will be among his family chatting. Myself and Bashir will stay and discussed in the room later fell asleep and called it a day. I remembered one day while we were eating food Bashir observed that I did not leave the rest of the food for him, he wisely wants me to remove my hand then he said "you are the senior leave me, to finish it". I did so since eating what we like in the house was never a problem.

A friend of Sarkin Fulani in neighbouring Niger republic invited him for a function all of us in the household engaged in preparation for the journey we the young ones engage in slicing the feathers of fowls and other simple errands we ate and drank even before the take up journey. Ducks, guinea fowls, chickens and small animals were slaughtered and fried for the journey of Sarki to Niger republic for the function. This is where we bid each other goodbye as when he will return by then I would have return to Kabobi.

In this village I saw a woman that was buried mistakenly thinking she had died. I saw the woman as the villagers were claiming that she was resurrected from the dead and come out from the grave and her tongue was tight now as she cannot speak anymore. Rationally, however, how can an ordinary mortal be death and resurrected, it is unjustifiable. What is possible the woman lost consciousness and cannot recover on time while those close to her did not check properly and rush takin her to the grave while alive. To an average villager the woman came back from heaven to accomplish certain mission. My religion teacher informed us man dies ones, once you die, you have gone forever and he gave us cogent reasons but from the scriptures and reasoning. In one of his teaching he reasoned with us that let everyone of us ask himself where are his death grandfathers as they died have anyone of us ever seen them coming to greet you even once? Secondly, ask your parents have they ever witness any of their relations or friends coming back from the grave? I thought of this and reflected our religion teacher was right. We die once.

Death of Our Leader Malam Aminu Kano 1983

As I returned to Kabobi my friends were so happy to received me back. Bashir in Dankama missed a friend and a brother as I left. In addition, we have no phones in our house likewise in Dankama there was no phone services. He will miss me as we played together, ate together, slightly fought, read together, prayed together, worked together, went on errands together, and we shared one mother together my Gwoggo, above all we slept nearby as his mat close to mind. This world is wonderful, it brings us together and forcefully separate as it likes. I left Dankama too with nostalgic feeling. How I wish we sometimes control certain situation so that we can make reasonable adjustments.

The memories of Dankama lingered on me more than of my father's land Matsai. Perhaps why I never care to have worries and nostalgic feeling about Matsai is perhaps because it is my land where my father and the fathers of my fathers were born and died. The land I have been coming and will continue coming in as much I am alive and able. In addition, the friends I had in Matsai did not enticed me and penetrate my hearts like those in Dankama and Kabobi. All those while I do not have any feeling of going back to Funtua or boarding house in Kagoro. I thought as for Funtua the one that always attract me to home was no more, she died. Had it been she was alive, I will have longed for hear and longed for her love, dishes and care. My mother was loving and protective, I missed her. My brothers do not support me much most of them bullied me with punches and tongues calling me with names I hate. In the boarding house eventhough I like school, as I want to qualified to be like Mr Inuwa K. Bahago our determined Principal however, some senior boys bullied us by confiscating our properties. One worrying thing that continue to disturb me was how my new iron bucket bought by my father was confiscated I later saw it with my name SANI GARBA boldly written yet the senior boy in the central taps fetched his water and left with it. In Magaji Kabobi, his household members, most members of the community and my young friends I found truth and loving friends. I prayed the holiday may long and long and long till eternity.

My returned from Dankama introduced a new chapter of my vacation as everything that has a beginning must have an end. The tail end of my stay in Kabobi had come. I turned my attention on getting my hedgehogs and Magaji reasoned with me, he wanted to please me. Some of the courtiers were assigned to get it for me I was comfortable as some of the courtiers were my friends. They never look at me as a small boy but discuss with me and ask about my school and my father. Some people wonder why this town boy, became bush boy to ask for bushiya instead of cow, bull, ram, goats, hare, fowls, pigeons, or even horse. I do not care let everyone face his business my teachers from home, Tsangaya, and western schools taught me to focus on my needs in as much as it will not transcend on the needs of others. The concept of Ummah is above a person was instilled on me, and I believed with it. My people are above me, even the home training and what our scholars are training us on is that one should see himself as part of the large society and should struggle to keep it one and to help in building it.

I was rounding off my visit as some days remained for me to go back to Funtua and then to the boarding house. In the palace of Magaji one morning as we finished discussing while listening to radio which was by his side. The announcement was made that a renowned politician, party leader, scholar of repute and revolutionary personality Malam Aminu Kano was dead. The leader of the talakawa as he was referred to led a formidable national party that was socialist incline called Peoples' Redemption Party (PRP). Most of us big and small like his party because it manifestoes concentrated on freeing the talakawa who have no much were mostly poor and were large in number and were oppressed and oppressed by the few elites. The man although never succeed in becoming Nigerian president in 1979 and 1983 democratic elections in Nigeria, he however succeeded in checking the excesses of some rulers – kings/emirs and other government officials. Secondly, he succeeded in organizing the downtrodden to fight for their rights get education and become enlightened. His party succeeded in winning only two states, so they had two states Governors in Kaduna and Kano.

Another major contribution and achievement of this leader was in promoting women education. He opened Madrassa in Kano and educated women this helped in opening more Madrassa in Kano and other parts of Nigeria. He will be likened to leaders like late Chairman Mao Tsetung, late President Julius Nyarere of Tanzania, late President Nelson Mandela of South Africa, President Mahathir Mohammed of Malaysia, the Singapore leader and many of them who put their people above themselves. I once saw late Malam Aminu Kano in one village Dungurawa, a Fulani settlement in Dambatta district of Kano state while I escorted my step mother on visit to her parents in 1980. As he climbed the drum to lecture the political gathering he spoke in Hausa language and quoting verses from the holy Qur'an that emphasized on fairness and justice since then I started to like the man. Later I used to follow their political campaigns in radio, television and newspapers. There was time he came to Funtua but I did not see him when later I went to township stadium they had finished. Adieu Malam we really missed a sincere leader, nationalist and promoter of fight against injustice. According to his major biographer who wrote the book Malam Aminu Kano: Time and Life of an African Revolutionary. Malam was a classroom teacher before joining partisan politics and he rose to become a PRP national leader for the whole of Nigeria. He led by example.

PART FIVE

My Hedgehogs

Some few days to my holiday end in Kabobi the hedge hedgehogs arrived. An aide of Magaji by name Rabo got it for me from his farm. As stated these people are predominant farmers, while few joint farming with other types of businesses and trade like blacksmithing, carving, petty businesses such as selling of meat, rearing for payment. Exactly, two days to my going as the five rodents were brought my new Mummy as well as my step grandmother collected them in order to ensure their safety before my transit. Therefore, she took them while I felt comfortable I got what I wanted. I was congratulated as I was happy really for that. As the rodents were with her seeing what she was to me and what she was to Magaji I felt confidence that on my journey day they would be parked and caged in an empty carton.

Unfortunately, bad news emanated that my hedgehogs were missing in the night probably. Was it a conspiracy by someone or some people in the Magaji's household to frustrate me and spoil my happiness. They conspired, I thought the way I had observed them discussing while looking at me. When I passed them pounding in group they will be laughing. I did not report my suspicion to Magaji but felt more uncomfortable indeed. I had the confidence that whatever God destined to be my own will be mine. They gave excuses such as hedgehogs were spirits and they said no matter how you cage these rodents they will run away in the night.

It was commonly believed and mostly discussed in the village as I heard them exchanging views that hedgehogs dance in the night as late famous Hausa singer Shata song a song for her as some claim it has spirit. Some added that no matter the heaviness of the mortar you cage the rodent on it will run away in the night. These views did not convince me, and I never intend to go and ask my teacher of Science and any Religious teacher. It may be some of the villagers had really observed something related to hedgehogs as they kept on discussing the spirit nature of the hedgehogs. Magaji was so worried I lost my hedgehogs, and he was so much worried that I am now no longer so friendly and sociable as before. I looked at the women as no longer friendly and my respect for them reduced.

My friends supported me and had my similar thinking and we all were convinced that something bad had happened to the hedgehogs and we taught that the women probably slaughtered them and ate them up. The women in my discussion with them they kept on querying me what will I do with hedgehogs they knew that I do not know how to eat them and I cannot rear them as the rodents are wild species. I never care and my answer perhaps never convince them. Why should they have conspired against me, afterall by extension I am their grandson and grandson of their loving husband. I looked at them as wicked and inconsiderate to give me such a parting gift.

My journey back to Matsai was on Monday so that I will be handed back to my relatives that come to Kagadama market. I bid goodbye to Kabobi and to close friends – Rabi'u and Abdullahi. I once more thank Rabo the courtier that brought me the hedgehogs and he ensured me to take heart. Magaji Kabobi kept on supporting me and ensuring me to take heart. Bye - bye Kabobi till another time. In the market I stayed with Magaji in his court till evening time when the brother of my father Baba Halilu will come and pick me to Matsai garin Damau. I ate and drank fura to my fill. Some of the Kabobi villagers that came to the market asked me about my hedgehogs and some sincerely commiserated with me as my close friends did. I imagined how I will meet Matsai after leaving for about two weeks really time flies. I thought how our boarding house would be as I was away this while. I promised myself to remain resolute no matter the defeative tendencies women that stole my hedgehogs wanted to push me into. I got many gifts such as pigeons, fowls, and cash from friends and relatives in Kabobi and Dankama gave me. Traditionally, all the gifts were handed over to my father's brother who took everything. We the children were not allowed to be holding money except some coins for cheap sweets, kuli- kuli and biscuits. I like the culture because it helps in discipline for the younger ones.

Back to Matsai

We reached Matsai in a transit tractor used for transportation during dry season. How we sat in the tractor truck was an arrangement of face –me I – face use. I did not enjoy the journey atoll, however, there is nothing I can do. The tractor was the one on queue to carry passengers and goods. The road from Kagadama to Matsai was full of sand and up and down. The tractor's truck trailed the body and turning anywhere the driver turned it. This transport to me is what I can call no choice because I cannot trek about seven kilometers from the market to Matsai. The passengers were parked some with animals crying and squeezing people some chickens complaining. Moreover, the road as I said was not friendly atoll. I wondered while in the cities we boarded fords buses with comfort, some people use even more comfortable cars like the Peugeot GR cars as my father had one he bought in 1982 while here buses and lorries that deserve to be off the road were the main transport means. At most in a car like that of my father only five persons where allowed to be boarded at a time.

When I returned Galadima welcomed me back together with his family. To have many relations is good. Within a short span of time I was taken to Kabobi, Dankama and coming back to Matsai where I started. My friends were happy to see me back and in good health, on my side I was happy when I went to Lawal's family house to meet him. His mother was in the house she welcomed me to the house. Women in Matsai went out with their tuluna to fetch water in faraway wells and boreholes. Even the wives of my grandfather were not spared they also went to the well with their tuluna. As a result, they protect their water very well by covering the small mouths of the tuluna to avoid insects, lizards and similar dirts going inside. These water containers made water to be cool especially during heat season. There were no refrigerators in Matsai to cool water these tuluna replaced the refrigerators in most cases. The culture of women going out to fetch water surprised me immensely. I looked how on earth they will not ask us to go and fetch the water for them. I have been coming to Matsai to see my brothers but water seem to be exclusively in the confine of women. In Funtua no matter the shortage of water I have never seen my mother or my step mother going out to the water sale point in Zaria road or to neighbours wells to fetch water even on a cup or jug.

It was a political time therefore, political activities were on top gear as second round of national elections were to take place the major political parties were: National Party of Nigeria (NPN), Unity Party of Nigeria (UPN), New Progressive Party (NPP), Peoples' Redemption Party (PRP) and Great Nigeria People Party of (GNPP). The campaigns trained came to Matsai and environment as I returned I saw the ongoing popular event in the village was politics. The prominent politician in the village Malam Barau Matsai was a strong supporter and official of NPN the popular party in most places in the Northern Nigeria. My friends were now going round to campaigns by selling the names of the candidates in various areas of the Matsai like Unguwar Malamai, Unguwar Arewa, central area, Radi, Buluskore, Kabobi, 'Yenhoho, among others. Malam Barau name from time to time will be heard as chanted by boys led by Arma as you will hear Malam Barau Matsai NPN in the air piercing the early night mood. Malam Barau Matsai was a kingmaker but they were chanting his name all over the village like a contestant.

I will soon go back to Funtua as I was told by Galadima. Already I learnt that my father had send a message that I should return like this as school will soon resume. Luckily enough Galadima supported me to still enjoy my wild adventure in the village. In Matsai we moved around like ants, we were always busy with our business. Sometimes going to the stones area sides northward, sometime going eastward taking Kagadama road, sometimes going toward graveside sometime following westward toward market upto

Babbarruga road. I have never climb the stones of Matsai even to see the shapes of hand and footprints on top, I never satisfy my curiosity as to explore more. The stones are historically significance as they serve as a shield by the first settlers of Matsai against raiders. Sometime I and my friends especially Dandare and Lawal we will go to Fadama side where tomatoes, pepper, Guava, mango, garden eggs and other vegetables and fruits were cultivated. I remembered I experimented grafting on one guava in our relative farm. I cut one sweet guava bud and join with another bud (branch) of the other I then tied as we were taught in school by our Integrated Science teacher.

When one thinks of how Matsai was peaceful, less sophisticated and almost zero crime village, I will wish how Funtua would be so? Myself, Dandare and Lawal will sleep outside Galadima's home feeling no fear of attacks, thefts, Shafi mulera or any evil that will attack us. As you know the village stands in savanna therefore, the wheather is usually hot this time of April through July our room was unbearable therefore we came out to save ourself from the heat.

Galadima arranged for my journey back to Funtua, my father's brothers Ibrahim Sarkin Tasha was billed to escort me to Katsina where I will stay enroute to Funtua. My father will later come to Katsina then I will follow him back home. In Saulawa quarters where we had a house built many years by my father's stepfather and brother Late Saje Isyaku a Native Authority sergeant from Matsai a very good and considerate man. I lodged in the guest room and my friends Ahmadu, and Iro especially joined me. This house is significance in my life. It was in the house that I was born on Friday, 1968. Whenever, we come to Katsina the house is where we lodge.

Katsina City 1983

I stayed for about two days expecting my father to come and pick me. My stay in Katsina gave me a chance to visit my relatives such as: my nearest aunt Gwoggo Ta'alkali, my mother's relation Hajiya Mainika, Gwoggo Zuwaira and Gwoggo Tashinkafi at Kofar Marusa quarters. Katsina is a big city where you can move without reaching its ends easily unlike Kabobi or Matsai village where you can easily reach the end of the village. I went to Unguwar Alkali quarters, to Kofar Sauri qurterss, to Kofar keke quarters. There are supermarkets, big garage, Libraries, hospitals, clinics, big mosques and churches, stadium, television station, fire brigade office, big and regular markets, police station, schools, higher institution, prisons, the government reserve areas (GRA), and many infrastructures. My father told me it was a Province during colonial time before independence in 1960, now it was a Local Government Council.

My schedules in Katsina was to go round the city like an independent tourist seeing different historical and monumental artifacts. Ahmad especially was more close to me, we therefore moved with him to see the city. I have an inquisitive mind that like to find out and discovered. In Gobarau minerates the curator guided us to climb the stairs and see for ourself. It was said the Katsina people of the 14th century use the minerates of this mosque to spy and see who were coming to attack them and how the territory was. According to a popular legend going round in Katsina and part of Hausaland in those years from the Gobarau minerate one can see Ka'aba in Saudi Arabia. I look at the minerate which was only less than fifty metres length. Why one will not easily deny their views when they put it forward is that Katsina was home to famous scholars in Islamic jurisprudence. The famous scholar Almghili was said to have been to Katsina and had a school where he taught. Our Scholars and Historians made us to believe that there were many real saints that were in the community. Why this phenomenon of sainthood exist may be linked to their knowledge and the fear of God by some of the great scholars like Danmarina, Dantako and many of them were claimed to have existed here.

Two famous graveyards were name after the two prominent saints the most popular one in the southern part of Katsina in Kofar Kwaya side named Danmarina it was said that the saint was born right in the grave yard. According to narrators of the legend a pregnant woman was dead and buried as medical technology in our country has not reach a stage of conducting caesarian to bring baby from dead women, the woman after sometime gave birth in the grave. The boy grew up and was visiting dyeing industry nearby to play discover the environment. The dyers traced him to the grave and that was how he was discovered. Furthermore, it was said when he was taken to famous Tsangaya for schooling he performed wonderfully by easily memorizing everything recited to him. The boy was nicknamed Danmarina. He grew up and became famous scholar and revered to a position of a saint.

The other famous scholar was Wali Dantako who also live in Katsina city, a scholar of repute and had many followers. As was popularly known as narrated by the historians this famous scholar was a contemporary of Wali Danmarina but live in different part of Katsina city at the time. Probably, Waliy Dantako resided around southern part of Katsina city as graveyard named after him was adjacent to main general hospital, road to Kofar Sauri quarters. One legend that really fascinated me was a debate that ensued between these two emeritus scholars, it was said that Wali Dantako threw a moon shaped carved from calabash to the sky and it look like new brand moon of Ramadan of that year. As some historians claimed the rivalry led to Wali Danmarina pointing at the moon and said "if the moon is really the moon of Ramadan fast from Allah let it remain". It was said it quickly fell down. This rivalry sometimes was more or less among the followers of the scholars than from the scholars themselves as in most cases we tend to be very fanatical and follow wishful thinking than reasons. On the other hand, some scholars play with the intelligent of their followers, especially when they discover their followers are ignorants to the core.

In Sabonlayi quarters of the city most of the structures that may catch a visitor to the area are the hotels and brothels spread all over. We went there to see for ourself. There was music both in the daytime and above all in the night. Our Malam had already warned us of the consequences of going to earn sin where the brothels reside, we avoided that. The night life I enjoyed it as we use to go to the cinema which was near our house. The Rex cinema was near us therefore whenever I was in Katsina I will follow my relatives from Matsai and Maidankundi among others to go and watch films – Chinese, Indian, American. We usually like Chinese films as they showed styles of fighting and how they respect master or teacher. It was during Eid festivals we met in Katsina to celebrate together. As part of our tradition and religion for instance, after each year's Ramadan fast ends on Eid or Sallah day people gather to pray on the next day a grand durbar would be held. Our people from Matsai, Dankama and Kabobi also travelled to Katsina and participate in the durbar. The durbar used to remind me of war time as the procession of the emir of Katsina passed with security carrying arms. One particular sound that was traditional herd on a day after Sallah was an iron gong (kuge) they beat to tell everyone that emir was set to go. I asked my father who enlightened me about the traditional sound called kuge. He told me even during communal wartime kuge was used to gather warriors for the planned expedition.

Home Sweet Home

Unexpectedly, my father came to Katsina for the weekend and other family issues, I immediately gathered my property so that I will not be caught unaware because I will follow him to Funtua. Already, I started to made arrangement for going back to boarding house. In one A.D. Saude supermarket I bought a one tin of powder milk. In boarding house eventhough the government of Kaduna State was doing well in feeding us like in the morning of Mondays tea and bread, lunch jollof rice, in the night yam. In the night we will be given rice for the dinner. I met everyone in good health. My grandmother was happy to see me back hale and hearty, I knew I will be asked many questions about my journey and people of Matsai, Kabobi and Dankama – the deaths and the ones living.

My grandmother had retentive memory to remember everything wherever she went to or once lived. I wondered what a gift. Even her stay in Wagini village where she married Malam the father of Maliki she told me. What is more interesting her journey to Mecca and her stay in the Holy City I enjoyed staying with her because of her wisdom, hardworking, storytelling and listening skills. I brought goriba, kanya, Yakuwa(a hibiscus type of plant) use for food and medicine, and above all the birds – pigeons that I cherished. The pigeons too, like the hedgehogs I had to shed tears later as they were eaten up by others that I never catch. Is this our household members at that time or the birds flied away to join their kind in another house? The answer was beyond me. The prime suspect were two women - Gwoggo Fara and Gwoggo Baka that spoke to me about the missing pigeons, the way they talked to me at that time there was mischief in their tunes and almost laughing.

In the early evening after we finished our dinner as it was a Tsangaya free day I came to grandmother where I met my step sister Assibi sitting. As usual I know I would be really interrogated and luckily enough I can recall everything from my journey to and from. My grandmother principally asked me of Malam Barau Matsai that prominent politician who ushered us into the Marmaru festival sport arena in Matsai. I narrated everything about him to her. When I finished she told me he was her stepson. Exactly, what happened when their father late Shantali died in the late 1940s he left Malam Barau, Malam Yakubu, Malam Suleiman among others therefore, they were small and then entrusted to the wives of their senior brother in which my grandmother was one of the wives. I told her about my hedgehogs and how they got missing she sympathized with me and smiled. Grandmother was always a friend and very sympathetic when it comes to something happening to us. When I told her about the Matsai market and its fallen glory she danced her head and breathed an air of regret and sympathy and informed us that in those days the market was big and attracted people from far and near. I wonder what is causing this type of misfortune and retardation. I asked myself is it lack of the ability of people of Matsai to economically accommodate people coming to their land for trading. Or is it government lack of seriousness to provide infrastructures in the market vicinity and the whole village in general. I also taught, is that lack of water that drove people away to the once flourishing market. Whatever, the answers to these series of questions something went wrong and its need to be corrected now or in the future. My eyes were heavy already I was clutching my blanket and on my favourite corner in her sitting room the sleep defeated me. The chain of the narration shall definitely continue and continue with the probing eyes of grandmother.

Sometimes I detested going to farm because of the lack of much care by my senior brothers along the way, in the farm and on our return journey. The usual thing was that our father will give us transport fares to and from the farm. Sometimes we look for free ride to the farm along Mairuwa road on the main road to Gusau city. Upon all the bullying I enjoyed taking ice cream from the saved transport fares. We were buying the ice cream cup at the price of twenty kobo (20k). In the farm we broadcasted fertilizers during rainy season, harvest maize when it was cut and other petty jobs to keep us busy and teach us the value of labour and specifically farming. Our father like farming and he encouraged us to go to farm. We grew maize, guinea corn, beans mainly in our farms. Sometimes we grew other cash crops such as groundnuts, cotton and soybeans. My father can be described as a successful farmer as he had many farms and sometimes even grew tubers for our consumption. But what disturbed me was that he was unable to own a tractor ploughing machine, harrowing machines and related. He was subsistence farmer anyway, who farms fifty bags and below far year. What I also observed he gave zaka of one bag out of every ten, and gave some of the bags as gift to relatives and friends. The zaka and gift I always feel happy with them as they are means of helping others. When the price of the crops rises like in July or there about he will sale some. As a government worker this farming was helping to sustain him and his family.

In the farming business of our father I was fully involved I can remember I have been going to the farm since I was six years old. The time I was just there as an observer because there was nothing substantial I can do. To attract me which made me to go to the farm was to ride on a motorcycle of my father to the farm. Secondly, before going to farm with me we will branch at Malam Bale's shop a nearby canteen and my father will buy coke, fanta and bread which we will carry to the farm. I enjoyed drinking these sugary foods during break time in the farm.

Sometimes in the morning we will go to the nearby grazing fields and feed the sheep belonging to my grandmother. Usually the three shepherds include me, my grandmother and Assibi. The grazing land were then abundant plots of people not yet developed so we will take the sheep there going round freely the vast land. Assibi was denied western education and I it was the support of grandmother and her mother that caused it. My grandmother made cheese for us whenever one of the sheep gives birth I enjoyed eating the cheese she made with the first milk of the animal. I was very elated and eager to eat the cheese that she professionally fry. Generally, I enjoyed staying with grandmother but one must work she was not lazy therefore when you are with here you cannot be lazy.

In the night before going to bed, I told her my journey to Dankama. Grandmother told me the mother of the late Sarkin Fulani was our relation. In addition, the first wife of the Sarkin Fulani I met was our relation. Also my father when his father died he was taken there by his aunt the then wife of late Sarkin Fulani. She told me how he suffered in Dankama, he passed through rough, dangerous and risky life of rearing the family horses in the bush as small as he was. Definitely as she was narrating it will anger one. How on earth can sensible people leave young boy with beast to rear and in the bush with no much care being an orphan does not mean to be subjugated to hardship and neglect. Probably, those who knew her and knew the background of the boy in Dankama and Matsai among the friends and relatives informed her and this compelled her to arranged immediate visit to Dankama at that time where motors were few most of the journey they did by walking the long distance on one's feet. As she alarmingly told us the condition she met him in Dankama was not appealing. From then he was returned to Katsina and put under the care of yet another relation and kinsman late Saje Isyaku a Colonial serving police officer who really did his best in taking care of him. It was later that my father in his usual admonition he uses to inferred on us he narrated by corroborating what grandmother said about his life in Dankama and in Katsina with Saje Isyaku of blessed memory. He worshipped his stepfather, he was so loyal to him that he even transferred the loyalty to his family.

Life in Funtua during holiday revolved round going to Tsangaya to farm and back home. Sometimes in the night when it was Thursdays and Fridays or during tashe we gathered outside to do meru, langa, sing or do other children plays around our houses. No fear of anything. Sometimes we preferred to stay with grandmother and listen to her tales and sometimes we also contribute by narrating one tatsunniya or the other that sometime we badly narrate them incomplete or fabricate. Abdu my step brother who later came to our house from another village was many years ahead of us so since he was in higher class in Shehu primary school he used to tell us about stories of Prophets of God, companions of our Noble prophet peace of God be on him and stories of Saints their Islamic studies teacher taught them. I enjoyed listening to their stories as I realized there were lessons that one must learn and must put them into his life in order to be good person. Grandmother was vast sometime she too will tell us about the wonderful stories of Saints and Prophets sent to humankind and the Jinns.

Life with grandmother was wonderful as she taught one to be for all to benefit others. Her service to the community was her motherly roles as the neighbours around held her as mother and leader they came for advice. When some pregnant women were to be put to bed she assisted and serve as midwife. Although, her role as midwife my father frowned at that to the extent he asked her to stop as sometimes late in the night she will be asked to attend to a woman in labour. I do not share the views of my father atoll to her stopping the midwife role. One thing that I enjoyed was the meat of rams heads from the proceeds of her labour that those family she attended to during seventh day they gave her. It was a tradition that they give the heads, legs, skins and add a calabash full of grains with clothe and sometimes money.

She used to tell us about life in Wagini village after the demise of her first husband. She remarried Malam after her takaba. According to grandmother they lived in Wagini village for quite a long time where she traded and gathered money through making foods such as kosai, daddawa and related businesses. With her husband they set for Saudi Arabia to perform hajj and stay there to look for greener pasture. This happened when there was no available aeroplanes services for all to go to Mecca for the religious rite. Our pilgrims who unofficially travelled followed through Borno in Nigeria they will then entre Port Lomé in Chad from there to some villages traversing sahara in a dangerous journey that only few survived. As she was narrating I became very fearful. 'To the extent that we use to see corpses of humanbeings on the sand of the sahara abandoned some had become skeletal". I wondered really. She told us how drinking water was very scarce that they had to ratio it to survive on the desert. They stayed in some villages along the routes to farm, rest and look for money to reimburse their provision. According to some historians some Hausa people from Nigeria stayed and lived in Sudan and became citizens as a result of this Hajj by road. Furthermore, the Sahara has its criminals too that kill and confiscate the property and cash of travelers whenever they attack. It is risky following the routes in the sahara especially by few people like how our grandmother cross it at that time.

It was in the Sudan fort that they will cross the Red sea in one of the biggest ship that carries men and their properties. She told us how she was almost thrown into the sea as she fainted in the ship. Immediately the travelers cross the Red sea Mecca will welcome them. Grandmother finally made the journey with her husband. Likely, the difficult life my mother went through made her to be different person like most of our people in Nigeria who only want to be given by begging. She coped with the life of takari in mecca, as illegal aliens they were highly chased by the Meccan's officials. According to her if the officials catches one he will be imprisoned and deport to Northern Nigeria. Two basic things took them to Mecca, first looking for greener pasture, second to perform Hajj. She succeeded in the latter, the first she did not get as she told us she was working in Mecca as menial labourer on farms and wash in houses of the residents.

Funtua to Kagoro

As the holiday ends already I bought cabin biscuits, powder milk, sugar, gari that we soak with water and sugar and sometimes with kuli –kuli we made salad with. Also I bought canned fish, roasted groundnuts, cornflakes, with doughnuts given by my aunt. To make me enjoy and stay in the school comfortably also two roasted chicken were also included in my provision. Alhaji Bala was our escorter as he was hired by our parents to take us from Funtua to our schools in his brand new commercial commuter hiece bus. My senior brother was dropped in Government College Kaduna, I missed my brother later we passed Kaduna and followed Sabon tasha to Kachia road bush everywhere with dots of hamlets and villages here and there. In the bus we were not many. Our next stop was in Samaru Kataf where another girl by name Maryam was alighted and ushered in into the boarding house for girls.

We reached Fadan Kaje village where another student was alighted and received by the school officials of Government Secondary School into the boarding house. Malam Bala as our guide and our driver hopped in and he drove us to the main road our journey continued until we reached Kagoro. Right from Mararraba a junction outskirt of Kagoro town my chest started to pounced the warning came to me I will be left to myself as I am sure my friends will not return to school until next week or there about. I was disturbed. We reached the school along Kafanchan road I was helped to remove my big iron box and other property from the bus. I bid them good bye until another holiday in August of that year. I entered our hostel – Harling house where I met only few students. My father was very restrictive and like us to be educated therefore, he does not joke with our education. All these miles we covered was in former Kaduna state. Infact, from Dankama to Jaba town (kwoi) that is end to end then. Malam Bala will take the last girl on our bus to Government Girls' Secondary School, Kwoi in

Jaba district. Our parents were so organized and cared very much for our future that they organized themselves to entrust us on Malam Bala to safely brought us to our schools from Funtua. The driver was a father to us he was very protective and disciplined no joke and he held the trust with utmost honesty as our parents negotiated with him we did not care to touch our pocket monies the responsibility to settle him rested with our fathers. I longed for him immediately I was left alone. Unfortunately, for me Cletus, Tuska, Halliru, Mustafa, Lawal, Yusuf my close friends were not yet back to school like me.

My Pentagon

My daily rituals revolved round the five places in the boarding house in Kagoro. Firstly, the dormitory where I rest and took my baths and prefer for class. Secondly, the school mosque where I prostrated and prayed to God five times a day. Thirdly, dining hall where I received my meals – breakfast, lunch and dinner. It is here I got energy to walk, run, work in the hostel during cleaning, and read. Fourthly, classroom where teachers like Mr Mahingoda taught me English. Finally, the bush where I use to hibernate to run from bullying of the exerting senior boys especially during weekends. I cannot describe myself as any significant game and sport participating student, however I represented my house (dormitory) in the School Interhouse Sports in the category of sub –junior. Also I love games and sports because regularly I went to watch hockey, basketball, pole-vault, long jumps, high jumps, shot – put, javeline, football, and other track games. Our school excelled in most games and sports within the Southern zone of Kaduna state. One thing that impressed me eventhough I am not a major stakeholder in the school as far I leadership and sports are concerned but when decision was made that we were to sacrifice our meat for somedays to buy game and sporting materials. We forgone the consumption of the meat and got balls, nets, bats, rakes, javeline, jerseys, tables, etc.

The dormitory named Harling house with our recognized yellow colour is adjacent to red house and opposite to blue house. I learnt that they are the oldest dormitories in the school. Later other new dormitories were built in the northern part of the school. Harling house have about twenty four rooms constructed facing each other. In each room there are three (3) to four (4) double bunk iron beds, that are made to contain six (6) to eight (8) students. Sometimes squatters or friends of the senior boys joined them in a room to make it crowded. We the junior boys were sleeping on top. I was lucky I am not bed wetting otherwise I would have suffered as I observed others do. To make it worse our lavatories are outside I fear coming out in the night to urinate. What is more difficult at that time was we have to go to bed at 10:00pm after coming back from prep. The housemaster and the house prefect will have checked us to make sure everyone was around then bell would be rung for every student to sleep. Notwithstanding, some miscreants senior students would not be around on their beds. Some of the miscreant students were said to be going to brothels, bars and on unofficial travels. Early in the morning around 5:00 am we have to be woken up for morning prayers the Christians will go the school chapel while the Muslims will go the mosque. Whenever I heard the bell waking me up, I felt disturbed as if not to wake up. No way if one dare stays on bed the prefect will punish him. Immediately after the morning devotion to the God all of us the junior ones will come back and assemble for the sweeping and washing of our environments. All of us the junior students must participate if one dodges he will be punished later because there were supervisors who report to the house prefects.

The school mosque was very close to the dining halls and to our sport arena, we said all our prayers in the mosque. The Imam who led us in prayer resided in Kafanchan town a distance of about ten kilometres. When he was not around like during the morning prayers and the night prayers the learned senior boys led us in prayer. The rule of the school was that all junior students must be wearing shots, therefore during prayers we were however allowed to wear long trousers. One thing I like with the programmes of the mosque was the constant admonishing and preaching spearheaded by the Muslims Students Society officials of the institution. We will be in the mosque listening to their admonishing and preaching that I found interesting and use to console me. Some of us were in the habit of hanging around the mosque to dodge certain work in the dormitory the senior boys use to check and chase anybody found. When I prayed as I communed with God I got relief from home sickness and bullying of the senior ones.

Time for breakfast usually commenced around 7: 15 am. Immediately we finish sweeping and other morning environmental cleanliness we will go for our baths, brushing our mouths and get prepare for class. During cool seasons we had to go to class without bath as we cannot take bath with cool water with the excessive cool wheather of Kagoro at the end of the year. We usually looked at Kagoro mountain bringing out white smoke. In the dining halls we the junior ones we received our tea and breads in the junior hall while the senior students received theirs in their separate hall. Tickets were issued to us and the food prefects together with prefects on duty that day will coordinate the cooking and the distribution of foods to all of us under the food master. When a student comes to collect his ratio the column for the breakfast will be ticked. During lunch time it will be same this is to avoid collecting double ration by some of us. Upon all these measures sometimes if our provision end and were not fully satisfied we ventured to go for collecting double by craftily cleaning the marking on our meal tickets. Sometimes some of us were caught doing this kind of cheating and the prefects will punish one but usually mildly since it is a matter of food and hunger.

Our senior master Mr Mai'unguwa coordinates activities in the school. There was a time we missed our meal in the afternoon this great man rushed in his corolla wagon car to his house or a canteen outside the school as he came back with a bag of rice that the cooks immediately cooked for us. The teachers like us and were so caring, I cannot remember any bad habit they meted to me or my colleaugues. Mr Lekwot our guardian master was very authoritative personality indeed but caring and he encouraged us to read in the library during Library hours. Mr Mahingoda regularly when he was on duty he will come to test our food to make sure the quality of the foods are standards. Most of us disliked Tuesdays dinner where our evening meals use to be tuwon Alabo and okra soup we instead abandoned the food and eat our provision. Sometimes we were given pap with kosai as breakfast. The cooks were active and were under the tutelage of chief cook most of them they took us as their children. Our dining halls also serve as our theatre where dramas, quiz competitions, debates and other important cultural and important gatherings are held. On Thursday during dinner we eat pounded yam and a boiled egg. During fasting periods since the cooks were from far area in Kagoro and Kafanchan towns our senior MSS officials will cook the sahur meals for us. The food during sahur will be much for us we use to reserve some for our Christian friends. More interestingly, whenever it was Ramadan some of the catholic students will join us to fast from dawn to dusk. I like the blend of Idris morrow bread that we were given to take our tea with. The school management and the students leaders were very honest that we felt safe, secured and we were all protected irrespective of our nature. Similarly, the local people - the Kagoro people were very accommodative.

My classmates in class 2F that we usually interact include: Gambo Lawal, Mustafa, Halliru Ubangida, Yohanna John, Ali Umaru, Tuska Danbaki, Iliya Umar. We were many admitted that year because the class stream of form two students starts from 2A – 2H about eight or even more classes. Mr Mahingoda was our favourite teacher he taught us English language, he so much care about our learning. He will ask us to read a paragraph of a passage myself and some of my friends he will ask us to read and as we read poorly he will roar teasingly- "Sani Garba ba Turanci, Gambo Lawal ba Turanci, Ali Umar ba Turanci…". He will continue listing the full names of our types until we were laughed upon and felt embarrassed. Fortunately, enough for me Mr Mahingoda became my friend and my father, therefore as he recognized me in the school and in the class in particular I became serious in learning.

There was a book programme introduced by the management during that time and we were asked to pick a novel to read and return. The first English novel I was given to read at that time was *Hopeful lovers* published by Macmillan Nigeria under the pacesetters series. This programme helped all of us to develop our English vocabularies. In addition, there was Library hours that we went to library to read. I became versed in Shorthand subject as I was lucky my senior brother did commercial subjects he gave me some of his textbooks. Our library was located adjacent to the administrative block is a rectangular single building fully equipped with enough shelves heavy with all the subjects taught in the school and other information resources needed by us. The library staff controlled us while in the library and our monitor recorded those that misbehave. I like our library, and I will confidently say the school management did well by inculcating the reading culture on us right from our teens. The Motto of our school is – truth shall prevail. I witnessed truth really prevailed in the school.

On weekend especially on Sundays I and my friend Mustafa after taken our breakfast of we will quickly vamoose into the bush near the school premises to run away from bullying. We took risk going to the bush as there were harmful reptiles such as snakes and also those hunting rats, and birds were scattered all over. It was a lucky day for us one day otherwise the hunters will have pierced their arrows on our bodies. We usually climbed the mango tree in our usual venue we heard noise the hunters followed bird as it escaped to our tree. We quickly alert them about our presence to avoid being wounded or killed.

We have to rush to the bush and hide otherwise the senior students will give us heap of their clothes to wash, plates to wash and all sorts of chores. Additionally, if one is unlucky if he makes slight mistakes he will be punished either frog jump, beating or riding a vespa or any nasty punishment they are good at. Sometimes if we were broke enough there was no cabin biscuits or any provision with us we will sneak to come back and receive lunch of bread and soup as we said our prayers we will went back into the bush stealthily avoiding the eyes of the seniors. Sometimes when one was unlucky he will be caught and no excuse. The only thing for one is to resort to prayer to God for a soft landing. As junior students we were like slaves we do not have our freedom, our time was subjected to what our senior wishes except during official hours like lessons, compulsory sports, afternoon or night preps among others. To be a junior student was to be a slave and one must prefer for a life of slavery. Infact, even our properties were threatened by the senior students. This made some of us the junior students to dislike school. Whenever we returned for a new school term we will start counting the days to holiday because of unfriendly nature of most senior students. Sometimes I had to bribed one bully in our dormitory with my provision to be free from his wickedness. Unfortunately, you cannot complain to the school authority not to your parents no one will support you. The only consolation from our families and others was one day you will be the senior. My main sport was marathon or long distance running, before I was playing ball and hockey later I stopped it. I only cherished marathon jogging. This sport is so easy for me, even when the school authority made it mandatory for us to go for early morning jogging in the field I was not disturbed. I liked it and I can endured it.

Glossary

Aci balbal – Local lamp, that does not have glass cover

Adaka – A box.

Agadas – A city in Niger republic.

Alabo – Yam powder use to make amala similar to tuwo is eaten with Soup or stew.

Alaramma – A title given to someone who memorizes Qur'an and he keeps on writing it.

Allah – God the Almighty.

Alkali – A judge.

Ardo – A Fulani chief in – charge of small area.

Ba – No, that is there is no…

Babbar riga – Big gown usually wear by Hausa, Yoruba people and other parts of Africa.

Barawo – Thief

Bedi – Neem tree

Burukutu - Also spell as burkutu, a local alcohol made from grains usually guinea corns.

Bushiya – Common name for hedgehog in Hausa.

Daddawa – Local condiment made from locust beans use for soup and other dishes.

Dambu – A food similar to couscous, use to be cook through steaming.

Danmarina – The child links to dyeing pits or dyeing industry.

Danwake – Food made from beans sometimes mix with corn or cassava groundnut oil is use to eat it.

Durbi – A title for the district head of Mani in Katsina State, Nigeria.

Fadama – Water logged area where basically vegetables, fruits, crops and related farming are done. Some call it irrigation.

Faranshi – People of our village and neighbouring areas referred to all residents of France colonized areas of Niger republic as Faranshi

Fulbe/Fulani – People that are usually nomadic in Nigeria they are not in our land but in other states like Bauchi, Adamawa, Sokoto, Gombe, Borno.

Fura/Hura – A drink made from millet powder in our village mostly mix with

milk.

Galadima – Higher ward head assisting Shantali

Gardawa – These are mostly unmarried senior male students in Tsangaya school that are put in charge of the junior ones.

Gawo – A big tree that have fruits which animal rearers feed their animals with.

Goriba – A tree of palm trees kind that produces medium time fruits that are usually tasteless and sometime low sugared taste.

Gwoggo – An aunt from the father's side

Hajiya – A title traditional assigned to female person that went to Mecca and performed hajj.

Illo: name of male usually used by Niger republic people and those Sokoto state, Nigeria

Islamiyya – Modernized form of Tsangaya where mostly children are taught Qur'an recitation, exegesis, jurisprudence, Arabic language among others.

Jinns – the spirits. That cannot be easily seen in their real form except in rare cases.

Kaba – Fibre of shrub kind, use to manufacture mats, fans, boxes, hats, etc.

Kanya – A tree commonly found in the savanna areas of the Northern Nigeria that have sweet and sour taste fruits that have also four to three stony like seeds inside.

Kada – Cotton.

Kambulti – night spirit

Kofar Kwaya – One of the gate in Katsina city through which you can entre.

Katsina from north/south axis. It is our main gate we entre the city from Funtua.

Kofar Sauri – One of the famous gate in Katsina city named after *Sauri* a royal officer. Through this gate you follow to Matsai, Dankama and many villages.

Kosai – A sort of cake made from paste or sauce of beans.

Kuli – kuli – A sort of candy made from groundnut use to make salad

Kurna – A kind of fruit similar to a lote shrub fruit but larger than lote shrub fruit.

L'ecole – A Primary School as called in French.

Labi – Animal path approved by the constituted authorities.

Langa – a kind of sport where one can hold up one of his leg and lift his body with one at the same time pushing his rival and his rival pushing him.

Madrassa – An Islamic school where teaching of the religion and sometimes vocation is taking place

Magaji – Ward head.

Magarya – Lote shrub that produces sweet and sour fruits.

Malam – An Islamic cleric who is versed in some aspects of the religion. Or even any teacher in any type of school.

Malama – Female teacher

Marmaru – A festival of harvest era usually celebrated at the end of the year.

Matoya – Pottery industry

Meru – hide and seek play.

Nono – Sour milk.

Pullako –A word describing bravery, self deprivation, shy feeling, patriotism, firmness, etc.

Ramadan – The 9th month in Islamic calendar that Islamic faithfuls fast

Sahur – A meal taken in the late night by muslim who wants to fast.

Sabon fegi – New quarters or new housing area.

Sarki – An emir or king

Sarkin Samari – A leader of the youths.

Saje - Sergent

Shafi mulera – A cult group that are said to be stealing genitals and other parts of human body.

Sharo – A culture where youngmen whipped each other in an arena.

Takaba – Waiting the women that that their husbands die do for four lunar months and ten days. This is to confirm pregnancy and complying with the Islamic law even if the woman is aged.

Takari – An illegal alien

Talakawa – The poor people

Tatsunniya – fable or tale which are usually fabricated stories in order to teach a lesson.

Tsagewa – A nicknamed for Alaramma Muhammadu, that is who beats well to the extent that the whip marks appear on student body.

Tasha – Motor garage

Tashe – Holidays the Tsangaya schools go during some Islamic festivals or graduation.

Tsangaya – An Islamic school sometimes referred to as Madrasat where Qur'an is taught by the erudite Islamic scholars to mostly children and youths.

Tuluna – Earthen water containers, spherical in form. Some call them Pitchers

Turanci - English

Turare - Balm tree, long and scently.

Tuwo – A local dish made from grains such as guinea corn, millet powder/flour mostly eaten by the Hausa

Ummah – Community/ Society.

Waina – A food similar to bread but spherical and usually smaller made from grains powder.

Waliyi – A saint.

Yadi – Derived from 'Yard', it is referred to a Department of Public Works and Services in Funtua.

Yakuwa – A sour vegetable plant use to make salad or principally soup.

Yara – A market square, where petty traders sale: foods, tea, and related activities are carried out.

'Yentare – These were group of buyers/traders that intercepted traders coming to Matsai and bought from them the wares they intended to bring to market.

Zaure – Sitting room/reception in typical Hausa house, this is where guests are received and household members rest as well.

Table of Contents

I want morebooks!

Buy your books fast and straightforward online - at one of world's fastest growing online book stores! Environmentally sound due to Print-on-Demand technologies.

Buy your books online at

www.morebooks.shop

Kaufen Sie Ihre Bücher schnell und unkompliziert online – auf einer der am schnellsten wachsenden Buchhandelsplattformen weltweit! Dank Print-On-Demand umwelt- und ressourcenschonend produzi ert.

Bücher schneller online kaufen

www.morebooks.shop

KS OmniScriptum Publishing
Brivibas gatve 197
LV-1039 Riga, Latvia
Telefax: +371 686 204 55

info@omniscriptum.com
www.omniscriptum.com

Printed by Books on Demand GmbH, Norderstedt / Germany